God Is Not a Christian

ALSO BY DESMOND TUTU

Made for Goodness

An African Prayer Book

God Has a Dream

No Future Without Forgiveness

Rainbow People of God

Crying in the Wilderness

Hope and Suffering

God Is Not a Christian

Speaking truth in times of crisis

Desmond Mpilo Tutu

Edited by John Allen

RIDER

LONDON • SYDNEY • AUCKLAND • JOHANNESBURG

1 3 5 7 9 10 8 6 4 2

Published in 2011 by Rider, an imprint of Ebury Publishing
First published in the USA in 2011 by HarperOne,
an imprint of HarperCollins Publishers Inc

Ebury Publishing is a Random House Group company

The Random House Group Limited Reg. No. 954009

Addresses for companies within the Random House Group can be found at
www.randomhouse.co.uk

A CIP catalogue record for this book is available from the British Library

The Random House Group Limited supports The Forest Stewardship
Council (FSC), the leading international forest certification organisation.
All our titles that are printed on Greenpeace approved FSC certified paper carry the
FSC logo. Our paper procurement policy can be found at
www.randomhouse.co.uk/environment

Mixed Sources
Product group from well-managed
forests and other controlled sources
www.fsc.org Cert no. TT-COC-2139
© 1996 Forest Stewardship Council

Printed and bound in Great Britain by CPI Mackays, Chatham ME5 8TD

ISBN 9781846042515

Copies are available at special rates for bulk orders. Contact the
sales development team on 020 7840 8487 for more information.

To buy books by your favourite authors and register for offers, visit:
www.randomhouse.co.uk

God bless our world

Guard our children

Guide our leaders

And give us peace

For Jesus Christ's sake.

Amen

—*Adapted by* DESMOND TUTU *from a prayer by*
TREVOR HUDDLESTON

Contents

FOREWORD

Some of my friends are skeptical when they hear me say this, but I am by nature a person who dislikes confrontation. I have consciously sought during my life to emulate my mother, whom our family knew as a gentle "comforter of the afflicted." However, when I see innocent people suffering, pushed around by the rich and the powerful, then, as the prophet Jeremiah says, if I try to keep quiet it is as if the word of God burned like a fire in my breast. I feel compelled to speak out, sometimes even to argue with God over how a loving creator can allow this to happen.

When I recently announced my retirement from public life, I said I wanted to slow down and spend more time reading and writing, praying and thinking, and being with my family. I also said that, apart from continuing some of my activities as a Nobel Peace laureate, I would adopt a lower public profile and no longer give interviews to journalists.

Reflecting on this collection of what I have said and written over the past forty years has shown me how difficult it is going to be for me to shut up (and reminded me how sexist my language was when I was young!). For as I see and read about the suffering, the pain, and the conflict that God's people still undergo, their experiences cry out for the passionate involvement of people of faith in advocating for the values of God's kingdom.

Yet no one is indispensable, least of all me, and what gives me hope and reassurance as I approach my eightieth birthday is the remarkable passion for justice and peace that I have experienced when meeting and speaking to thousands of young people around the world in these first years of the twenty-first century. When I see their level of commitment, I know that the world is in safe hands.

In the Church of Sant'Egidio in Rome, home of an extraordinary community of laypeople devoted to working for the poor, there is an old crucifix that portrays Christ without arms. When I asked about its importance to the community, I was told that it shows how God relies on us to do God's work in the world.

Without us, God has no eyes; without us, God has no ears; without us, God has no arms or hands. God relies on us. Won't you join other people of faith in becoming God's partners in the world?

—DESMOND TUTU, APRIL 2011

EDITOR'S PREFACE

If the reasons for Desmond Tutu becoming one of the world's most prominent advocates of faith-based social justice and religious tolerance could be reduced to a single, succinct statement, it would be this: his fierce and uncompromising determination to tell the truth as he sees it.

In the early years of his public life, his courage in speaking out, angrily and fearlessly, against apartheid at a time when most of South Africa's political leaders were in jail, exiled or banished, or facing torture and assassination made him a hero in the eyes of most black South Africans. But, as Nelson Mandela would later write, it also made him "public enemy number one" to most whites—the reviled subject of death threats and even, it became clear later, serious attempts on his life.

That changed after the release of Mandela and the transition to democracy, when Tutu became as watchful a critic of his friends and erstwhile allies in the struggle against apartheid as he had been of their predecessors in government. At the same time, he used his anti-apartheid credentials to broaden his campaign for justice and human rights to Africa and the world, in situations of political injustice and oppression ranging from Marxist Ethiopia and Western-aligned Zaire to the Middle East and Panama under military rule.

He did not stop there: the values underlying his advocacy—drawn from his faith and the vision of a shared humanity held out by the African spirit of *ubuntu* ("a person is a person only through other persons")—led him to become a campaigner against intolerance in general, speaking out for interfaith understanding and cooperation, and against religious fundamentalism and the persecution of minorities such as gays and lesbians. His outspokenness and his readiness to voice what appeared on the surface to be heresy have made him both an admired icon and a lightning rod for controversy—a man who could be acclaimed the hero of a crowd on one day and be forced to remonstrate with a murderous mob on another.

Watching him exercise his ministry over the course of thirty-five years, whether in the streets and stadiums of South Africa—rallying people's morale with stirring rhetoric, channeling anger in creative directions, and defusing violence—or in closed meetings with dictators, Western leaders, or Zionists angry at his identification with the Palestinians, I came to see that it is when he is faced with the toughest, most challenging situations that he is at his best. It is when he is called upon to deliver his most unpopular messages—sometimes to his opponents, at other times to his supporters—that he articulates his values, his ideals, and his faith most powerfully and persuasively.

I hope that this collection will reflect this face of Desmond Tutu. As a series of texts reflecting a life in action rather than the ruminations of a scholar, it comprises a disparate range of material: off-the-cuff interventions, answers to journalists' questions, letters, and both abbreviated and lengthy excerpts from speeches, sermons, and other writings, condensed and edited for clarity where necessary.

—JOHN ALLEN

God Is Not a Christian

PART ONE

Advocate of
Tolerance and Respect

Chapter 1

God Is Clearly Not a Christian

Pleas for Interfaith Tolerance

Nothing epitomizes Desmond Tutu's radicalism (using the word radical, as he likes to say, in the original sense of getting to the root of an issue) more than his views on the relationship of his faith to the faiths of others. This chapter combines remarks he made over four occasions, revealing a refreshing, inspiring, and, yes, radical perspective that has become particularly pertinent to the post-9/11 world.

1

This is an excerpt from a sermon preached at St. Martin in the Fields Church on Trafalgar Square, London, during a meeting of leaders of the world's Anglican churches after the fall of the Berlin Wall and the end of the Cold War, drawing on the Christian scriptures as the basis of his approach.[1]

I sn't it noteworthy in the parable of the Good Samaritan that Jesus does not give a straightforward answer to the question "Who is my neighbor?" (Luke 10:29). Surely he could have provided a catalogue of those whom the scribe could love as himself as the law required. He does not. Instead, he tells a story. It is as if Jesus wanted among other things to point out that life is a bit more complex; it has too many ambivalences and ambiguities to allow always for a straightforward and simplistic answer.

This is a great mercy, because in times such as our own—times of change when many familiar landmarks have shifted or disappeared—people are bewildered; they hanker after unambiguous, straightforward answers. We appear to be scared of diversity in ethnicities, in religious faiths, in political and ideological points of view. We have an impatience with anything and anyone that suggests there might just be another perspective, another way of looking at the same thing, another answer worth exploring. There is a nostalgia for the security in the womb of a safe sameness, and so we shut out the stranger and the alien; we look for security in those who can provide answers that must be unassailable because no one is permitted to dissent, to question. There is a longing for the homogeneous and an allergy against the different, the other.

Now Jesus seems to say to the scribe, "Hey, life is more exhilarating as you try to work out the implications of your faith rather than living by rote, with ready-made second-hand answers, fitting an unchanging paradigm to a shifting, changing, perplexing, and yet fascinating world." Our faith, our knowledge that God is in charge, must make us ready to take risks, to be venturesome and innovative; yes, to dare to walk where angels might fear to tread.

2

This talk also comes from a forum in Britain, where Tutu addressed leaders of different faiths during a mission to the city of Birmingham in 1989.

They tell the story of a drunk who crossed the street and accosted a pedestrian, asking him, "I shay, which ish the other shide of the shtreet?" The pedestrian, somewhat nonplussed, replied, "*That* side, of course!" The drunk said, "Shtrange. When I wash on that shide, they shaid it wash thish shide." Where the other side of the street is depends on where *we* are. Our perspective differs with our context, the things that have helped to form us; and religion is one of the most potent of these formative influences, helping to determine how and what we apprehend of reality and how we operate in our own specific context.

My first point seems overwhelmingly simple: that the accidents of birth and geography determine to a very large extent to what faith we belong. The chances are very great that if you were born in Pakistan you are a Muslim, or a Hindu if you happened to be born in India, or a Shintoist if it is Japan, and a Christian if you were born in Italy. I don't know what significant fact can be drawn from this—perhaps that we should not succumb too easily to the temptation to exclusiveness and dogmatic claims to a monopoly of the truth of our particular faith. You could so easily have been an adherent of the faith that you are now denigrating, but for the fact that you were born here rather than there.

My second point is this: not to insult the adherents of other faiths by suggesting, as sometimes has happened, that for instance when you are a Christian the adherents of other faiths are really Christians without knowing it. We must acknowledge them for who they are in all their integrity, with their conscientiously held beliefs; we must welcome them and respect them as who they are and walk reverently on what is their holy ground, taking off our shoes, metaphorically and literally. We must hold to our particular and peculiar beliefs tenaciously, not pretending that all religions are the same, for they are patently not the same. We must be ready to learn from one another, not claiming that we alone possess all truth and that somehow we have a corner on God.

We should in humility and joyfulness acknowledge that the supernatural and divine reality we all worship in some form or other transcends all our particular categories of thought and imagining, and that because the divine—however named, however apprehended or conceived—is infinite and we are forever finite, we shall never comprehend the divine completely. So we should seek to share all insights we can and be ready to learn, for instance, from the techniques of the spiritual life that are available in religions other than our own. It is interesting that most religions have a transcendent reference point, a *mysterium tremendum,* that comes to be known by deigning to reveal itself, himself, herself, to humanity;

that the transcendent reality is compassionate and concerned; that human beings are creatures of this supreme, supra-mundane reality in some way, with a high destiny that hopes for an everlasting life lived in close association with the divine, either as absorbed without distinction between creature and creator, between the divine and human, or in a wonderful intimacy which still retains the distinctions between these two orders of reality.

When we read the classics of the various religions in matters of prayer, meditation, and mysticism, we find substantial convergence, and that is something to rejoice at. We have enough that conspires to separate us; let us celebrate that which unites us, that which we share in common.

Surely it is good to know that God (in the Christian tradition) created us all (not just Christians) in his image, thus investing us all with infinite worth, and that it was with all humankind that God entered into a covenant relationship, depicted in the covenant with Noah when God promised he would not destroy his creation again with water. Surely we can rejoice that the eternal word, the Logos of God, enlightens everyone—not just Christians, but everyone who comes into the world; that what we call the Spirit of God is not a Christian preserve, for the Spirit of God existed long before there were Christians, inspiring and nurturing women and men in the ways of holiness, bringing them to fruition, bringing to fruition what was best in all.

We do scant justice and honor to our God if we want, for instance, to deny that Mahatma Gandhi was a truly great soul, a holy man who walked closely with God. Our God would be too small if he was not also the God of Gandhi: if God is *one*, as we believe, then he is the *only* God of all his people, whether they acknowledge him as such or not. God does not need us to protect him. Many of us perhaps need to have our notion of God deepened and expanded. It is often said, half in jest, that God created man in his own image and man has returned the compliment, saddling God with his own narrow prejudices and exclusivity, foibles and temperamental quirks. God remains God, whether God has worshippers or not.

This mission in Birmingham to which I have been invited is a Christian celebration, and we will make our claims for Christ as unique and as the Savior of the world, hoping that we will live out our beliefs in such a way that they help to commend our faith effectively. Our conduct far too often contradicts our profession, however. We are supposed to proclaim the God of love, but we have been guilty as Christians of sowing hatred and suspicion; we commend the one whom we call the Prince of Peace, and yet as Christians we have fought more wars than we care to remember. We have claimed to be a fellowship of compassion and caring and sharing, but as Christians we often sanctify sociopolitical systems that belie this, where the rich grow ever richer and the poor grow ever poorer, where we seem to sanctify a furious competitiveness, ruthless as can only be appropriate to the jungle.

3

Tutu's most detailed theological argument for interfaith tolerance was made to fellow Christians in a 1992 lecture in memory of the Roman

Catholic archbishop of Cape Town, Stephen Naidoo, with whom
Tutu had worked closely in defusing conflict in the city in the 1980s.

M ost Christians believe that they get their mandate for exclusivist claims from the Bible. Jesus does say that no one can come to the Father except through him, and in Acts we hear it proclaimed that there is no other name under heaven that is given for salvation (John 14:6; Acts 4:12). Those passages seem to be categorical enough to make all debate superfluous. But is this *all* that the Bible says, with nothing, as it were, on the side of inclusiveness and universality, and does the exclusivist case seem reasonable in the light of human history and development?

Fortunately for those who contend that Christianity does not have an exclusive and proprietary claim on God, as if God were indeed a Christian, there is ample biblical evidence to support their case. John's Gospel, in which Jesus claims to be the exclusive means of access to the Father, right at the beginning makes an even more cosmic and startling claim for Jesus, as the Light who enlightens *everyone,* not just Christians (John 1:9). In Romans, St. Paul points out that everyone stands condemned as under sin before God—both Jew and Gentile (Romans 3:9). This, which is central to the teaching he intends to convey, is found in an Epistle focused on the wonder of God's free acquittal of all. God's grace, bestowed freely through Jesus Christ, would be untenable if there were no universality about sin. Sin involves, in Paul's view, the deliberate contravention of God's law. There is no problem about the Jew who has received the Torah and constantly infringes it. But what is the case with regard to the Gentile, the pagan who seems to be bereft of a divine law which he could break and so stand justly under divine judgment? If he has received no law, then he patently cannot be adjudged in the wrong before God. Paul then declares that the Gentile too has received the law which resides in his conscience (Romans 2:15). Every one of God's human creatures has the capacity to know something about God from the evidence God leaves in his handiwork (Romans 1:18–20); this is the basis for natural theology and natural law. Immanuel Kant spoke about the categorical imperative. All human creatures have a sense that some things ought to be done just as others ought not to be done. This is a universal phenomenon—what varies is the content of the natural law. Paul and Barnabas invoke the same principles in their discourse at Lystra, where they were thought to be divinities (Acts 14:15–17). In his speech before the Areopagus, Paul speaks about how God has created all human beings from one stock and given everyone the urge, the hunger, for divine things so that all will seek after God and perhaps find him, adding that God is not far from us since all (not just Christians) live and move and have their being in him (Acts 17:22–31). Talking to pagans, Paul declares that all are God's offspring.

An important hermeneutical principle calls us not to take Bible texts in isolation and out of context, but to use the Bible to interpret the Bible, thus helping to ensure that our interpretation is read *out* of the Bible in exegesis and not read *into* the Bible with our peculiar biases. A related principle calls us to ask whether what we are saying is consistent with the revelation that God has given of himself finally and fully (as Christians believe) in Jesus Christ.

What I have tried to say here is that the text "No one can come to the Father but by me" need not be interpreted to refer only to the incarnate Logos, for there was also the preexistent Logos, as the Gospel of John attests (John 1:1). This would then mean that the preincarnate Logos would lead people to the knowledge of God, a revelatory activity that antedates Christianity. Does not Hebrews assert that God in sundry times and in diverse manners spoke to the fathers in the past through the prophets (Hebrews 1:1)?

If this is not the case, we must ask some further awkward questions. Whose divine writ runs where that of the Christian God does not run? What is then the fate of those who lived before Jesus was born on earth? Were they totally devoid of knowledge of God? How could they be blamed for something about which they could do nothing? How could they have been expected to have knowledge of God through Jesus Christ long before Jesus Christ existed? Jesus himself holds the Law and Prophets—that portion of the Bible we call the Old Testament—as authoritative; that is, as revealing in certain respects the will of God, as when Jesus appeals to the creation narrative about the indissolubility of marriage (Matthew 19:3–6). He quotes it with approval when he exhorts those who are pharisaical in their call for external religious observances to discover what the text "I desire mercy and not sacrifice" means (Matthew 12:7). How could those who predated Jesus Christ have come to the knowledge of God as is now attested to by their acquaintance with the divine will unless we accept that the preincarnate Logos was active in God's world long before Christianity saw the light of day?

God is clearly not a Christian. His concern is for all his children. There is a Jewish story which says that soon after the episode of the drowning of the Egyptians in the Red Sea, while the Israelites were celebrating, God accosted them and demanded, "How can you rejoice when my children have drowned?"

The Bible makes the position of those who make sweeping exclusivist claims for Christianity even more untenable when we ask some further questions. What about Abraham? Did he have an encounter with God when he decided to leave his people to go where he knew not? Was it a delusion, or did he in fact discern some command? The existence of the people of Israel, ultimately the existence of the Christian church and our *heilsgeschichte*—our salvation history—proclaim that he was not deluded. What about Moses? Did he meet with God at the burning bush and receive a commission to go down to Pharaoh or not? It appears that his theophany was genuine, for the Exodus did happen and God gave his people the Torah and accompanied them in the wilderness for forty years, then took them into the Promised Land. If all this did happen, then which God was responsible, if not the God and Father of our Lord and Savior Jesus Christ? We claim as monotheists, in narratives such as those about Abraham and Moses, that it *was* possible to have an authentic religious experience in which people encountered God long before the Christian dispensation. This must surely mean that persons were able in some way, perhaps inscrutable to some but clearly due to divine graciousness, to come to God and to have a real and profound relationship with God many centuries before the advent of Christ.

That Christians do not have a monopoly on God is an almost trite observation. We would have to dismiss as delusion and vanity the profound religious and ethical truths propounded by such greats as Ezekiel, Isaiah, and Jeremiah; we would have to be willing to jettison, for example, the "suffering servant" songs. And how could Jesus claim to have come to fulfill and not to destroy what had been proclaimed and foretold in non-Christian scriptures and in the life of a non-Christian community?

And how can anyone hope to understand the New Testament, and thus Christianity, apart from the Old Testament? How can there be any validity in the typology of the New Testament where, for instance, Jesus is described as the second Adam, as our Passover, as the Son of David, as the Messiah, as the Rock, unless we concede that these adumbrations, these foreshadowings in the old dispensation, referred to authentic encounters with the divine? And how is it possible for God to have created human beings, all human beings, in his own image and not have endowed them all with some sense, some awareness, of his truth, his beauty, and his goodness? If the opposite is asserted, it would call into question the capacity of the creator. The Bible, as we have seen, asserts what seems the reasonable position: that all God's human creatures in some sense have the divine hunger referred to by St. Augustine in his famous dictum: "Thou hast made us for thyself and our hearts are restless until they find their rest in thee."

Once we are compelled by the weight of the evidence to concede that perhaps God somehow revealed himself to the Jewish people, and that it was possible in some sense for the Jewish people to have come to God, then it is quite unacceptable to make this a unique exception. After all, these same people were able to speak about non-Israelites as being called by God, as when Isaiah spoke of Assyria as God's rod to visit his anger on his recalcitrant people, or when he referred to Cyrus, a pagan non-Israelite king, as Yahweh's anointed, Yahweh's Messiah (Isaiah 10:5; 45:1–4). It would be difficult to make sense of the indictments of an Amos or a Jeremiah pronounced against pagan nations unless there was a sense in which they too came under the purview of Yahweh and were expected to know of the demands of Yahweh! It surely must be more sensible to maintain that God was, and is, accessible to all his human creatures and that people did have a real encounter with this God before the Christian dispensation. This surely does more honor to God's goodness, mercy, and justice than the opposite position.

To claim God exclusively for Christians is to make God too small and in a real sense is blasphemous. God is bigger than Christianity and cares for more than Christians only. He *has* to, if only for the simple reason that Christians are quite late arrivals on the world scene. God has been around since even before creation, and that is a very long time.

If God's love is limited to Christians, what must the fate be of all who existed before Christ? Are they condemned to eternal perdition for no fault of their own, as they must be if the exclusivist position is to be pushed to its logical conclusion? If that were the case, we would be left with a totally untenable situation of a God who could be guilty of such bizarre justice. It is surely more acceptable and consistent with what God has revealed of his nature in Jesus

Christ, and it does not violate our moral sensibilities, to say that God accepts as pleasing to him those who live by the best lights available to them, who are guided by the most sublime ideals that they have been able to discern. It is no dishonor to God for us to claim that *all* truth, *all* sense of beauty, *all* awareness of and desire after goodness has one source, and that source is God, who is not confined to one place, time, and people.

My God and, I hope, your God is not sitting around apprehensive that a profound religious truth or major scientific discovery is going to be made by a non-Christian. God rejoices that his human creatures, irrespective of race, culture, gender, or religious faith, are making exhilarating advances in science, art, music, ethics, philosophy, and law, apprehending with increasing ability the truth, the beauty, the goodness that emanate from him. And we should also join in the divine exultation, rejoicing that there have been wonderful people such as Socrates, Aristotle, Herodotus, Hippocrates, Confucius, and others. Isn't it obvious that Christians do not have a monopoly on virtue, on intellectual capacity, on aesthetic knowhow? And wonderfully, it does not matter. Is God dishonored that Mahatma Gandhi was a Hindu? Shouldn't we be glad that there was a great soul who inspired others with his teachings of *satyagraha,* who inspired the Christian Martin Luther King Jr. in his civil rights campaign? Do we really have to be so ridiculous as to assert that what Mahatma Gandhi did was good, but it would have been better had he been a Christian? What evidence do we have that Christians are better? Isn't the evidence often overwhelming in the opposite direction?

Don't we have to be reminded too that the faith to which we belong is far more often a matter of the accidents of history and geography than personal choice? If we had been born in Egypt before the Christian era, we would have been perhaps worshippers of Isis, and had we been born in India rather than in South Africa, the chances are very, very considerable that we would have ended up being Hindu rather than Christian. It is worrisome that so much should be made to depend on the whims of fate, unless it is to make us more modest and less dogmatic in our claims. God can't want people to be Christians and then seem to stack the odds so very considerably against them and then proceed to punish them for their failure. Such a God is too perverse for me to want to worship him. I am glad that the God I worship is other than this.

We must not make the mistake of judging other faiths by their least attractive features or adherents. It is possible to demolish the case for Christians by, for instance, quoting the Crusades, or the atrocities of the Holocaust, or the excesses of apartheid. But we know that that would be unfair in the extreme, since we claim them to be aberrations, distortions, and deviations. What about Francis of Assisi, Mother Teresa, Albert Schweitzer, and all the other wonderful and beautiful people and things that belong to Christianity? We should want to deal with other faiths at their best and highest, as they define themselves, and not shoot down the caricatures that we want to put up. Many Christians would be amazed to learn of the sublime levels of spirituality that are attained in other religions, as in the best examples of Sufism and its mysticism, or the profound knowledge of meditation and stillness found in Buddhism. It is to do God scant honor to dismiss these and other religious insights as delusions, which they patently are not. We make ourselves look quite ridiculous, and our faith and the God we claim to be proclaiming are brought into disrepute. I have met great exponents and adherents of other faiths, and I stand in awe of them and want to take my shoes off as I stand on their holy ground. I have no doubt that the Dalai Lama is one such, and you can't but be impressed by his deep serenity, and the profound reverence that Buddhists have for life which makes them vegetarian, refraining from all killing, and constrains them to greet you with a profound bow as they say, "The God in me greets the God in you," a greeting which we Christians could make our own more truly since we believe that every Christian is a tabernacle of the Holy Spirit, a God-carrier.

To acknowledge that other faiths must be respected and that they obviously proclaim profound religious truths is not the same thing as saying that all faiths are the same, however. They are patently *not* the same. We who are Christians must proclaim the truths of our faith honestly, truthfully, and without compromise, and we must assert courteously but unequivocally that we believe that all religious truth and all religious aspirations find their final fulfillment in Jesus Christ. But we must grant to others the same right to commend their faith, hoping that the intrinsic attractiveness and ultimate truthfulness of Christianity will be what commends it to others. That as they see the impact Christianity has on the character and life of its adherents, non-Christians would want to become Christians in their turn, just as in earlier days pagans were drawn to the church not so much by its preaching as by what they saw of the life of Christians, which made them exclaim in wonder, "How these Christians love one another!"

I am not aware of any major faith that says human beings are made for a destiny other than the high destiny of being in uninterrupted communion with the divine, however this may be defined, whether the *summum bonum*, the greatest good, is to be absorbed into the divine, or to exist as distinct for all eternity in nirvana, or paradise, or heaven. I am not aware that any faith has declared that it is acceptable that human beings should be victims of injustice and oppression. On the contrary, we have been able to walk arm in arm with adherents of other faiths in the cause of justice and freedom, even as fellow Christians have vilified and opposed our witness.

I hope I have done enough to convince diehard exclusivists that the Christian cause is served better by a joyful acknowledgment that God is not the special preserve of Christians and is the God of all human beings, to whom he has vouchsafed a revelation of his nature and with whom it is possible for all to have a real encounter and relationship.

4

Tutu told students at the University of Khartoum on a visit to Sudan in 1989 that not only does he urge people of faith to practice tolerance and respect; he charges them that their faith requires them to act together in the cause of justice.[2]

P eople of religion have no choice in the matter. Where there is injustice and oppression, where people are treated as if they were less than who they are—those created in the image of God— you have no choice but to oppose, and oppose vehemently and oppose with all the force that you have in your being, that injustice and oppression. And so we can't help it if we oppose the obscenity of apartheid, which says that racism is the policy of a particular government. It isn't as if you sit down and say, "Do I want to, or don't I want to?" If you are a believer you must oppose injustice, whether you are a Muslim, whether you are a Christian, whether you are a Hindu or a Buddhist, because you see, this is one of the common factors in these faiths: not one of them has a low doctrine of human beings.

Christianity says human beings are created in the image of God; so does Judaism. Islam says you are the *abd,* the slave, of God whose purpose is to place your will in subjection to the will of Allah. And it says therefore that you are someone who can be in relationship with God. So each of these religions in its intrinsic nature compels its adherents to be people who strive for justice and for peace and for goodness. If you do not, in the face of injustice, stand up and oppose it, then every night you must confess and say, "God, I have sinned, because I have disobeyed a fundamental law of our relationship."

We do our religions scant justice, we put our religions into disrepute, if we do not stand up for the truth, if we do not stand up for justice, if we are not the voice of the voiceless ones, if we are not those who stand up for those who cannot stand up for themselves.

It is an incredible thing, that you have this convergence. If you look at how faiths speak of what is the destiny of humankind, we Christians say that the ultimate *summum bonum* is when we enjoy the divine vision, the beatific vision forever and ever, but we will remain distinct although in relationship with the divine Trinity. Islam also speaks about the time when we will enjoy absolute blessedness in the presence of the divine One. Don't Hinduism and Buddhism, having recognized that we are part of the divine, speak about *Tat tvam asi,* "That thou art," believing that if you can recognize what you truly are—that you are an aspect of the divine and ultimately will return to what you came from—you will be reabsorbed into the divine? All this speaks volumes about what human beings are.

CHAPTER 2

Ubuntu

On the Nature of Human Community

Desmond Tutu's stature as an exemplar of tolerance and inclusiveness among international religious leaders is rooted not only in his faith but in his understanding of the nature of human community, to which he brings a uniquely African sensibility. What follows is a compilation of excerpts from presentations made over three decades in settings ranging from South African newspaper columns to speeches abroad.

In our African *weltanschauung*, our worldview, we have something called *ubuntu*. In Xhosa, we say, "Umntu ngumtu ngabantu." This expression is very difficult to render in English, but we could translate it by saying, "A person is a person through other persons."[1] We need other human beings for us to learn how to be human, for none of us comes fully formed into the world. We would not know how to talk, to walk, to think, to eat as human beings unless we learned how to do these things from other human beings. For us, the solitary human being is a contradiction in terms.

Ubuntu is the essence of being human. It speaks of how my humanity is caught up and bound up inextricably with yours. It says, not as Descartes did, "I think, therefore I am" but rather, "I am because I belong." I need other human beings in order to be human. The completely self-sufficient human being is subhuman. I can be me only if you are fully you. I am because we are, for we are made for togetherness, for family. We are made for complementarity. We are created for a delicate network of relationships, of interdependence with our fellow human beings, with the rest of creation.

I have gifts that you don't have, and you have gifts that I don't have. We are different in order to know our need of each other. To be human is to be dependent. *Ubuntu* speaks of spiritual attributes such as generosity, hospitality, compassion, caring, sharing. You could be affluent in material possessions but still be without *ubuntu*. This concept speaks of how people are more important than things, than profits, than material possessions. It speaks about the intrinsic worth of persons as not dependent on extraneous things such as status, race, creed, gender, or achievement.

In traditional African society, *ubuntu* was coveted more than anything else—more than wealth as measured in cattle and the extent of one's land. Without this quality a prosperous man, even though he might have been a chief, was regarded as someone deserving of pity and even contempt. It was seen as what ultimately distinguished people from animals—the quality of being human and so also humane. Those who had *ubuntu* were compassionate and gentle, they used their strength on behalf of the weak, and they did not take advantage of others—in short, they *cared,* treating others as what they were: human beings. If you lacked *ubuntu,* in a sense you lacked an indispensable ingredient of being human. You might have had much of the world's goods, and you might have had position and authority, but if you had no *ubuntu,* you did not amount to much. Today, *ubuntu* is still greatly admired, sought after, and cultivated. Only someone to whom something drastic has happened could ever say, as a South African government minister once said, that the death of Steve Biko[2]—the death of a fellow human being—left him cold. That minister had lost his humanity, or was well on the way to doing so.

Westerners have made spectacular advances largely because of their personal individual initiative. They have made remarkable technological advances, for example. And yet that progress has come at a huge cost. The West's emphasis on individualism has often meant that people are lonely in a crowd, shattered by their anonymity. This is what makes it possible for people to pass by on the other side while someone is, say, being gang-raped: the passersby simply do not want to become too involved. People in the West have been brought up in a culture of success, where stomach ulcers become status symbols. There is an obsession with achievement, and it seems it does not much matter in *what* you succeed as long as you *do* succeed. The worst thing that can happen, it appears, is to fail. And that culture easily dismisses people as expendable, discardable, when, because they are poor or unemployed, they are judged to have failed.

Ubuntu teaches us that our worth is intrinsic to who we are. We matter because we are made in the image of God. *Ubuntu* reminds us that we belong in one family—God's family, the human family. In our African worldview, the greatest good is communal harmony. Anything that subverts or undermines this greatest good is ipso facto wrong, evil. Anger and a desire for revenge are subversive of this good thing.

CHAPTER 3

No Future Without Forgiveness

A Radical Program for Reconciliation

Desmond Tutu's advocacy of forgiveness by the victims of atrocity as a way to healing has repeatedly caused controversy, internationally as well as in South Africa, as the selections in this chapter illustrate.

1

The first time Tutu's views got him into trouble was during a pilgrimage to Jerusalem and Bethlehem over Christmas 1989.[1] During that pilgrimage, he visited Jerusalem's Holocaust museum, Yad Vashem, where he ended a comment in the guestbook with an appeal for God to "forgive all people who oppress others." This is what he then told journalists outside.

I think it's important for the world to be made to remember that we can sink to these levels. It is important also to be reminded that we all stand in need of forgiveness. My feeling would be to say, as our Lord would say, that in the end the positive thing that could come out of the horrors of the Holocaust—and also what comes from the prophets, your prophets—is the spirit of forgiving, not forgetting, the spirit of saying (and your martyrs used to say this too), "God, this has happened to us; we pray for those who made it happen. Forgive them. Help us to forgive and help us so that we in our turn will not make others suffer."

The Jews have a special vocation to be a light to the nations. I am proud of my Jewish antecedents, and I am able to stand up against the evil and injustice of apartheid largely on the basis of what I have learned from what we call the Old Testament but what is the Jewish scriptures. I pray, and I pray fervently, that the people of this land will be able to live in harmony and peace and happily with their Palestinian brothers.

2

The ensuing news reports saying that Tutu had called on Jews to forgive the Nazis led to a storm of criticism. Five months later, journalists in Cincinnati, Ohio, returned to the controversy after a meeting Tutu held with representatives of Reform Judaism. When those journalists asked him whether he believed that Jesus would have forgiven the Nazis if he had been a survivor of the Holocaust, Tutu offered the following reply.

Well, from the paradigm that Jesus provided, as he was being crucified, he said, "Father, forgive them." It wasn't as if he was talking about something that *might* happen. He was actually experiencing one of the most excruciating ways of being killed, and yet he had the capacity to live out a prayer that he taught Christians, that we can expect to be forgiven only insofar as we are ready to forgive.

In the Jewish scriptures, there is an extraordinary book, Second Isaiah, which contains a number of what are called "servant songs," uttered by the suffering servant of the Lord. Many of us have come to accept that those songs represent the pinnacle of an understanding of suffering. That is to say, you are not justifying suffering; you are not saying suffering is good. Suffering has to be eliminated as much as you can. But ultimately it appears as if the texture of the universe is such that good seems to require a capacity for suffering. You sometimes ask, Why is it necessary for a mother to suffer in order for there to be the great joy of the birth of a child?

You see, one often speaks out of an experience of suffering. The fact that I have a black skin already identifies me and singles me out for racist suffering. If black people were to say, "We cannot, we will not forgive white people forever," where would we be in South Africa? One is not speaking insensitively and one is not speaking as somebody who has not experienced suffering.

3

The next occasion on which Tutu's views landed him in hot water was later in 1990, during a conference called by South African churches—including both those which had supported and those which had opposed apartheid—after the release of Nelson Mandela and as negotiations on ending apartheid and establishing democracy were beginning. The purpose of the meeting was for church leaders to discuss how they might overcome their past alienation and work together in the future. This is an excerpt from Tutu's sermon opening the conference.

If there is to be reconciliation, we who are the ambassadors of Christ, we to whom the gospel of reconciliation has been entrusted, surely we must be Christ's instruments of peace. We must ourselves be reconciled. The victims of injustice and oppression must be ever ready to forgive. That is a gospel imperative. But those who have wronged must be ready to say, "We have hurt you by this injustice, by uprooting you from your homes, by dumping you in poverty-stricken homeland resettlement camps, by giving your children inferior education, by denying your humanity and trampling down on your human dignity and denying your fundamental rights. We are sorry; forgive us." And the wronged must forgive.

Those who have wronged must be ready to make what amends they can. They must be ready to make restitution and reparation. If I have stolen your pen, I can't really be contrite when I say, "Please forgive me," if at the same time I still keep your pen. If I am truly

repentant, then I will demonstrate this genuine repentance by re-
turning your pen. Then reconciliation, which is always costly, will
happen. Even when a husband and wife quarrel, until one of them
can say, "Sorry, forgive me," they can't really restore their former
relationship.

4

*A theologian of the white Dutch Reformed Church, which had pro-
vided theological justification for apartheid, responded by confessing
his and his church's responsibility for the policy and the suffering it
had caused. Tutu reacted in turn with this short comment.*

I believe that I certainly stand under pressure of God's Holy Spirit
to say that when that confession of wrongdoing is made, those
of us who have been wronged must say, "We forgive you," and then
together we may move to the reconstruction of our land. The confession is not cheaply made and the response is not cheaply made.

5

*The Dutch Reformed Church delegation endorsed the confession,
but leaders of the black churches that had been established by Dutch*

Reformed missionary work disputed both the sincerity of the delegation's declaration and Tutu's acceptance of the confession. Tutu defended his position.

I heard people say that I had no mandate in a sense to have accepted a confession on behalf of anybody except myself, and I believe that it is right for people to say so. It is the height of presumption for me to have suggested that I was speaking on behalf of anybody in a sense, though I need also to say that I have been ministered to by very many people in my life, and I want to give thanks to God for that.

Malusi Mpumlwana[2] stood up here to tell you about his experiences of detention and torture. When I was general secretary of the South African Council of Churches, Malusi Mpumlwana came to Johannesburg on one occasion. He has said here that he had difficulty forgiving, but I want to tell you that on that occasion he said, "You know, Father, when they torture you, you look on them and you say, By the way, these are God's children," and he said, "and you know they need you," meaning himself, "to help them recover the humanity they are losing." And he spoke out of that kind of pain, and I listened to him, as a young person ministering to me on the meaning of forgiveness.

I was part of a South African Council of Churches delegation when we went to Mogopa, a village which was being demolished and the people were going to be uprooted. The church leaders went to Mogopa to pray with the people before their removal. As we prayed in the rain at about midnight, one of the old men in the village whose home was about to be demolished, whose schools had already been demolished, whose churches and clinics had been demolished, stood up and prayed a prayer that I will never understand. The man said, "Thank you, God, for loving us." I have never understood that prayer.

And then I have been with men like Walter Sisulu[3] and others who have been in jail for twenty-five, twenty-seven years for having the audacity to say they are human. They come out of that experience and they have an incredible capacity to love. They have no bitterness, no longing for revenge, but a deep commitment to renew South Africa. I am humbled as I stand in front of such people; and so, dear friends, I think I am convicted by the Holy Spirit of God and by the gospel of our Lord and Savior Jesus Christ in offering forgiveness.

There are no guarantees of grace. When Jesus Christ looked at Zacchaeus the tax collector (Luke 19:1–10), he had no guarantee that Zacchaeus would respond to the grace of his forgiveness and love. We are people of grace who have to have the vulnerability of our Lord and Savior Jesus Christ on the cross. Jesus Christ, in accepting Zacchaeus, released Zacchaeus so that Zacchaeus could then say, "I will make restitution."

God has brought us to this moment, and I just want to say to you, I am deeply humbled, and I speak only for myself. I cannot, when someone says, "Forgive me," say, "I do not." For then I cannot pray the prayer that we prayed, "Forgive us, as we forgive."

6

Receiving an honorary degree in Benin in West Africa in 1991, Tutu
advocated that the values embodied in ubuntu *should be given prac-*
tical expression in African systems of justice.

I want us to see a resurgence, a revival, a renaissance of so many
of the wonderful attributes and values that Africa has. You know
we have had a jurisprudence, a penology in Africa which is not retributive. We've had a jurisprudence which was restorative. When
people quarreled in the traditional setting, the main intention was
not to punish the miscreant but to restore good relations.

For Africa is concerned, or was concerned, about relationship,
about the wholeness of relationship. That is something we can
bring to the world, a world that is polarized, a world that is frag-
mented, a world that destroys people.

7

A year after an estimated 937,000 Rwandans were killed by their
fellow citizens in the genocide of 1994, Tutu visited their Central
African country as part of a church delegation. In a series of sermons
and speeches, he urged Rwandans to break what he described as an
ongoing cycle of killing, as elites of the two major population groups,
the Hutu and the Tutsi, pursued a generations-long power struggle.
On the last morning of the visit, he went to a church at Ntarama,

south of the capital, Kigali, to which the government regularly es-
corted visitors upon whom it wanted to impress the horror of the geno-
cide. Without warning, Tutu and the party of evangelists in which
he was traveling were led into the dimly lit church, to find themselves
walking on the year-old corpses of massacre victims. Outside, Tutu
broke down sobbing. A short distance from the church, the group then
visited women who were establishing a "peace village" named for
South Africa's President Mandela. Back in Kigali, Tutu was called
upon at short notice to address the nation, in a meeting of parliamen-
tarians, government officials, and diplomats.

Today we visited Ntarama. I was shattered. I said yesterday that you had been through hell, that you had walked through the valley of the shadow of death. Sometimes it is difficult to believe that we human beings are capable of the kind of things we can do.

Any right-thinking person would want to condemn unequivocally all of that massacre and killing and genocide without qualification. We have said that we have come to express our solidarity with you in the agony that you have experienced. And really, we're struck dumb. We have no right really to speak. We come seeking to assure you of the love and caring and concern of God. Our God is a God who does not take a holiday, does not take a day off; our God is always there. We come not as omniscient know-it-alls trying to prescribe ready-made, blueprint solutions.

We have been amazed and give thanks to God for the fact that people who could have been provoked to engage in an orgy of reprisal and revenge have, remarkably, by and large been restrained.

We give thanks to God for all of you, our sisters and brothers who have been so traumatized, who have suffered to the extent that you have suffered and yet who have somehow been given the capacity to hold back your anger and your bitterness and your natural desire to take revenge. We thank God for you.

We want to say we agree that there must be justice, that those who are found guilty of having perpetrated these atrocities or instigated others should indeed be brought to justice and that their impunity should be ended. But then we want to say, as all of you want to believe, that justice cannot be the last word. As I stood at that site this morning, I thought, Here I am, a grandfather with four grandchildren—I have a wife, I have four children, I have four children-in-law, I have brothers, I have relatives. And if by an accident of history I had been born in this country, perhaps I too would be saying my wife, my grandchildren, my son-in-law, my mother-in-law, they have been killed.

I come as an African. I come as one who willy-nilly shares in the shame, in the disgrace, in the failures of Africa, because I am an African. And what happens here, what happens in Nigeria, what happens wherever, even though I am in South Africa, that becomes part of my history, part of my experience—just as the successes that happen in Africa, I share in those too, through my solidarity and participation in African-ness. And so, as an African, as a human being, and especially as a Christian, I speak to you: we are Africans; we are human beings; we are fellow Christians. Let us break the cycle of violence, the cycle of reprisal, giving rise to counter-reprisal, giving rise to further counter-reprisal, a cycle in which one is top dog, and underdog wants to become top dog, and underdog becomes top dog, and top dog who has become underdog wants to become top dog again.

People have waited many, many years to redress balances, and we pray, dear sisters and brothers, let us break this cycle; let us break this spiral. We went to the central prison[4] yesterday, and we must say the conditions there are a disaster waiting to happen. We hope the international community can help to ease that situation, but we are scared that resentment will build up on the part of one group, looking for the opportunity of getting its own back.

And so I make my appeal. Please, God, give me the eloquence, the right words that will be able to touch the hearts of our sisters and brothers in Rwanda, and outside Rwanda: that our sisters and brothers must know that there can be no future without forgiveness. There will be no future unless there is peace. There can be no peace unless there is reconciliation. But there can be no reconciliation before there is forgiveness. And there can be no forgiveness unless people repent. God, we pray:

> *Touch the hearts of your children in Rwanda, and those of your children of this land elsewhere; touch their hearts that they may know that they have only one motherland. Let them know that they have only one future—a common future.*
>
> *God, we thank you that we were able to see resurrection; we were at Good Friday at Ntarama, and then we moved a little ways away and there women were setting up the peace*

village named Nelson Mandela. We give thanks that out of the grave will rise new life. This is a beautiful land, God; these are beautiful people, God. Touch their hearts, please God; touch their hearts that they may know they are bound together as one. Touch our hearts, touch the hearts of the international community, that we may be generous as we help our brothers and sisters here to heal this land. God, we know that you love Rwanda. Bind their wounds. Bind them together. Make them one nation, one people.

CHAPTER 4

What About Justice?

Arguments for Restorative Justice

Desmond Tutu's willingness to forgive the perpetrators of apartheid faced its greatest test when President Nelson Mandela, inaugurated in 1994 after his African National Congress (ANC) had won the country's first democratic election, appointed Tutu the following year to chair South Africa's Truth and Reconciliation Commission (TRC).

1

Speaking to the American human rights activist Kerry Kennedy soon after delivering the commission's main report to Mandela in 1998, he explained that forgiving did not mean forgetting.

We should not be scared of being confrontational, of facing people with the wrong that they have done. Forgiving doesn't mean turning yourself into a doormat for people to wipe their boots on. Our Lord was very forgiving. But he faced up to those he thought were self-righteous, who were behaving in a ghastly fashion, and called them a "generation of vipers" (Matthew 23:33, KJV).

Forgiveness doesn't mean pretending things aren't as they really are. Forgiveness is a recognition that there is a ghastliness that has happened. Forgiveness doesn't mean trying to paper over the cracks. Forgiveness means that both the wronged and the culprits of those wrongs acknowledge that something happened. There is necessarily a measure of confrontation. People sometimes think that you shouldn't be abrasive. But sometimes you have to be to make people acknowledge that they have done something wrong.

2

The law that established the commission, passed by Parliament after intense negotiations between the country's new and former rulers, established three committees: one to conduct inquiries into and hold hearings on what the law defined as "gross violations of human rights" during the apartheid era, one to hear applications for amnesty from the perpetrators of crimes and to grant amnesty to those who had acted with political motives and told the truth about what they had done, and one to recommend policies for reparations and the rehabilitation of victims and their families. Tutu gave a retrospective reflection on the commission's work in presentations in London and Copenhagen after the commission had handed its final reports to the government.[1]

Most of the world—and many of us, for that matter—believed that we in South Africa were going to be overwhelmed by the most comprehensive disaster during the apartheid era and the transition to democracy after Mandela's release. There was no doubt at all but that we would be victims of the most awful bloodbath in a ghastly race war. Things had reached such a pitch in the early 1990s that when the daily statistics of the toll the violence was taking were announced and they said five or six or ten people had been killed, we actually would sigh with relief and say that it was *only* five, six, or ten people. We were up a creek, as they say. And then the world was amazed on April 27, 1994, to see those long lines of South Africans of all races snaking their way to the polling booths.

The skeptics and cynics said, "Yes, they have made a remarkable—indeed, almost miraculous—transition from repression to freedom and democracy, and they have done so remarkably peacefully; but just wait until a black-led government is in place. Then you will as sure as anything witness the most ghastly orgy of revenge and retribution, for the blacks have suffered much at the hands of the whites and they will surely want to get their own back."

Well, mercifully these prophets of doom were proved to be wrong when the world watched with wonder and awe as they saw the Truth and Reconciliation Commission process unfolding. Instead of the victims of so much unnecessary suffering baying for the blood of their tormentors, they amazed the world with their magnanimity, their nobility of spirit in their willingness to forgive those who had inflicted so much suffering on them.

The Truth and Reconciliation Commission

During the period preceding the elections, negotiators had to decide how to deal with the horrendous legacy of our immediate past. Some, especially of the apartheid regime, advocated that a general amnesty or blanket amnesty be granted to all so that—as they imagined—bygones would be bygones, so that the past would not hold hostage the present and future. Mercifully, we don't possess a fiat by which we can declare, "Let bygones be bygones," and they dutifully become bygones and go and lie down quietly. They have an uncanny capacity to return and haunt us. An unexamined and unacknowledged past finds all kinds of skeletons emerging from all sorts of cupboards to bedevil the present. Just ask General Pinochet.[2]

Santayana declared hauntingly, "Those who forget the past are doomed to repeat it." And general amnesty victimizes the victims a second time around by asserting either that what happened to them did not really happen or, worse, that it was of little moment; and so those victims are not able to experience closure and will nurse grudges and resentments that may have dire consequences for peace and stability as their anguish festers, and they may one day take their revenge.

Some others thought the easiest path would be to follow the Nuremberg trial option and arraign all who were known to have committed or were suspected of committing gross human rights violations. Nuremberg happened because the Allies defeated the Nazis and could impose what has been called victors' justice. In our case neither the apartheid government nor the liberation movements of the ANC and PAC[3] defeated their adversaries. There was a military stalemate. It is almost certain that the apartheid security forces would have scuppered any scheme at the end of which they might be indicted. And South Africa could not afford the long trials, nor could an already overburdened judicial system have coped.

So the negotiators opted instead for a principled compromise: individual amnesty, not general amnesty, in exchange for the whole truth relating to the offense for which amnesty was being sought. "Amnesty for truth?" many have asked in genuine concern. "But what about justice? Are you not encouraging impunity?" First, it is important to stress that this way of going about things was deliberately designed only for this delicate period of transition, ad hoc—once and for all. Far from encouraging impunity, this way of going about things stressed accountability, since the amnesty seeker had to admit committing an offense. Innocent people or those who claimed innocence obviously did not need amnesty.

Some complained that this was letting the perpetrators off lightly. Is this in fact so?

We all know just how difficult it is to say, "I am sorry." Those are some of the most difficult words in any language. I do not find it easy to say them, even in the privacy of our bedroom to my wife. We can imagine, then, what it must have meant to the perpetrators to have to confess publicly under the glare of television lights. Frequently the perpetrator had been a respected member of his community. This was often the first time even for his family to hear that this apparent paragon of virtue had in fact been a member of a police team that used torture on detainees routinely, or that he was a member of a death squad that assassinated as a matter of course those who were regarded as opponents of the vicious apartheid system. The stigma of such public shame and humiliation is a heavy price to have had to pay, and in some instances shocked spouses ended up divorcing their husbands.

But in using this argument we would in fact be thinking only in terms of retributive justice, whose raison d'être is to punish the perpetrator. There is another kind of justice: restorative justice, whose chief purpose is not punitive but restorative, healing. It holds as central the essential humanity of the perpetrator of even the most gruesome atrocity, never giving up on anyone, believing in the essential goodness of all as created in the image of God, and believing that even the worst of us still remains a child of God with the potential to become better, someone to be salvaged, to be rehabilitated, not to be ostracized but ultimately to be re-integrated into the community. Restorative justice believes that an offense has caused a breach, has disturbed the social equilibrium, which must be restored, and the breach healed, in a process through which the offender and the victim can be reconciled and peace restored.

Monstrous, Even Diabolical Deeds

There were many hair-raising revelations about the awful atrocities amnesty applicants committed:

> We gave him drugged coffee and then we shot him in the head. We burned his body and whilst this was happening— it takes six to seven hours to burn a human body—we were having a barbecue and drinking beer.

You wondered what had happened to the humanity of someone that he could be able to do this. Quite rightly people were appalled. They said people guilty of such conduct were monsters or demons. We had to point out that, yes indeed, these people were guilty of monstrous, even diabolical, deeds on their own submission, but— and this was an important *but*—that did not turn them into monsters or demons. To have done so would mean that they could not be held morally responsible for their deeds. Monsters have no moral responsibility. But even more seriously, it meant we were shutting the door to any possibility on their part of improving, and if that were so we should really shut up shop, because the Truth and Reconciliation Commission was based on the premise that people retained the capacity to change, that enemies could become friends.

Ubuntu (and so restorative justice) gives up on no one. No one is a totally hopeless and irredeemable case. We all, even the worst of us, remain the children of God. We all retain the capacity to become saints. For us as Christians the paradigm was provided by our Lord and the penitent thief on the cross. The thief had led a life of crime presumably until he was crucified. Some might be appalled at his death-bed repentance and conversion, but not God, whom we seek to emulate. "Be perfect, as your heavenly Father is perfect" (Matthew 5:48, RSV) is Jesus's exhortation. We are not able to declare categorically that So-and-So has a first-class ticket to hell. We shall be surprised at those we meet in heaven whom we least expected to be there, and perhaps also by those we do not find there whom we had expected to be there.

The Potency of Truth as a Healer

I myself had not expected so many quite wonderful things to happen as did in fact take place in the Truth and Reconciliation Commission. I recall one mother coming to testify about her son, who had disappeared without a trace. I will never forget her voice, with its anguish and deep distress: "Please, can't you find me even a bone of my child so that I can give even only that a decent burial." We were sadly not able to help her.

But there were other instances of people who had been abducted by the apartheid security forces and who had been killed and buried secretly. We were able from amnesty applications to obtain information that enabled us to find secret graves from which we exhumed the remains of those who had been abducted. At one such site the grave was opened and the family of the suspected victim was standing looking inside the grave with its remains when a young man in the group exclaimed, "That's my brother. I bought him those shoes." The positive identification had been made. The family now knew what had happened and experienced a closure as they were able to give their loved one a decent burial. Until then I had not known that truth could be such a potent healer.

On another occasion a young man came to testify before the commission. He had been blinded when the police opened fire in a black township. He related his story and at the end he was asked how he felt. This blind youth smiled and said, "You have given me back my eyes." There was, it seemed, a wonderfully therapeutic power in relating his story to a friendly and supportive forum. In officially affirming his story, his truth, the commission and thereby the whole nation was affirming him. That made him feel valued and appreciated, feel that somehow his suffering had not been in vain, that it had made a contribution to the "struggle" which had ended in victory for justice and freedom—and he had been part of this glorious thing.

A white Afrikaner[4] man had lost an infant son in an ANC bomb attack. He came to the TRC—one of the few white people who came to tell us their stories, as opposed to those who applied for amnesty—and amazed us all with his lack of bitterness and anger. He said something quite surprising, and in many ways very courageous even after the transition from apartheid to democracy. He said that if he was bitter at all, it was not leveled at the ANC who had killed his child, but at the apartheid government of mainly fellow Afrikaners, and he added that he believed that his son's death had contributed to the positive changes that were happening in our country. I said to him when he finished his testimony that our country did have some quite extraordinary people, and no wonder such miracles as our transition were taking place.

Another white man, a former South African Air Force officer, had been blinded by an ANC car-bomb attack on Air Force headquarters in one of Pretoria's main streets. Twenty-one people had been killed and two hundred and nineteen injured. The white officer, Neville Clarence, said he bore no grudge against the perpetrators. He did not oppose the amnesty application of Aboobaker Ismail, the main applicant responsible for planning the attack, who apologized for the civilian casualties. Clarence and Ismail shook hands and Clarence said that he forgave him and that they should work together for the common good of all. He later said it was as if they did not want to let go of each other. The picture of them shaking hands was on our television screens and blazoned on the front pages of our newspapers, and it spoke more eloquently than any words what the process of reconciliation was about.

Conclusion

I could multiply examples of the same kind of thing but need to say too that there were others who said that the truth made them want to see the perpetrators facing trial, and still others who refused to forgive, often because they claimed that the amnesty applicants had not told the whole truth.

What it all says is that forgiveness is never cheap, never easy, but that it is possible, and that ultimately real reconciliation can happen only on the basis of the truth. In reality, there can be no future without forgiveness, for revenge merely begets further violence, causing an inexorable spiral of reprisal, provoking counter-reprisals ad infinitum.[5]

> *For, in truth, in this world hatred is not appeased by hatred;*
> *hatred is appeased by love alone. This is the eternal law.*
>
> DHAMMAPADA[6]

CHAPTER 5

Our Glorious Diversity

Why We Should Celebrate Difference

As the world's memory of apartheid receded, Desmond Tutu responded to a stream of invitations to speak around the world on the practical implications of ubuntu. An excerpt from a speech to the United Nations Commission on Human Rights in Geneva in 2001 follows.

We inhabit a universe that is characterized by diversity. There is not just one planet or one star; there are galaxies of all different sorts, a plethora of animal species, different kinds of plants, and different races and ethnic groups. God shows us, even with a human body, that it is made up of different organs performing different functions and that it is precisely that diversity that makes it an organism. If it were only one organ, it would not be a human body. We are constantly being made aware of the glorious diversity that is written into the structure of the universe we inhabit, and we are helped to see that if it were otherwise, things would go awry.

How could you have a soccer team if all were goalkeepers? How would it be an orchestra if all were French horns?

For Christians, who believe they are created in the image of God, it is the Godhead, diversity in unity, and the three-in-oneness of God which we and all creation reflect. It is this *imago Dei* too that invests each single one of us—whatever our race, gender, education, and social or economic status—with infinite worth, making us precious in God's sight. That worth is intrinsic to who we are, not dependent on anything external, extrinsic. Thus there can be no superior or inferior race. We are all of equal worth, born equal in dignity and born free, and for this reason deserving of respect whatever our external circumstances. We are created freely for freedom as those who are decision-making animals and so as of right entitled to respect, to be given personal space to be autonomous. We belong in a world whose very structure, whose essence, is diversity, almost bewildering in extent. It is to live in a fool's paradise to ignore this basic fact.

We live in a universe marked by diversity as the law of its being and our being. We are made to exist in a life that should be marked by cooperation, interdependence, sharing, caring, compassion, and complementarity. We should celebrate our diversity; we should exult in our differences as making not for separation and alienation and hostility but for their glorious opposites. The law of our being is to live in solidarity, friendship, helpfulness, unselfishness, interdependence, and complementarity, as sisters and brothers in one family, the human family, God's family. Anything else, as we have experienced, is disaster.

Racism, xenophobia, and unfair discrimination have spawned slavery, when human beings have bought and sold and owned and branded fellow human beings as if they were so many beasts of burden. They have spawned the Ku Klux Klan and the lynchings of the segregated South of the United States. They have given birth to the Holocaust of Germany and the other holocausts of Armenians and in Rwanda; the ethnic cleansing in the Balkans and the awfulness of apartheid; and what we have seen in Sri Lanka, in Northern Ireland, in the Middle East, in the Sudan, where there has been a spiral of reprisals leading to counter-reprisals, and these in turn to other reprisals. Martin Luther King Jr. said, "Where the law of an eye for an eye obtains, in the end all will be blind. If we don't learn to live as brothers, we will die together as fools."

Religion, which should foster sisterhood and brotherhood, which should encourage tolerance, respect, compassion, peace, reconciliation, caring, and sharing, has far too frequently—perversely— done the opposite. Religion has fueled alienation and conflict and has exacerbated intolerance and injustice and oppression. Some of the ghastliest atrocities have happened and are happening in the name of religion. It need not be so if we can learn the obvious: that no religion can hope to have a monopoly on God, on goodness and virtue and truth.

Our survival as a species will depend not on unbridled power lacking moral direction, or on eliminating those who are different and seeking only those who think and speak and behave and look like ourselves. That way is stagnation and ultimately death and disintegration. That is the way of people in times especially of transition, of instability and insecurity, when there is turmoil and social upheaval, poverty and unemployment. Then people seek refuge in fundamentalisms of all kinds. They look for scapegoats, who are provided by those who are different in appearance, in behavior, in race, and in thought. People become impatient of ambivalence. Differences of opinion are not tolerated and simplistic answers are the vogue, whereas the reality is that the issues are complex.

We need so much to work for coexistence, for tolerance, and to say, "I disagree with you, but I will defend to the death your right to your opinion." It is only when we respect even our adversaries and see them not as ogres, dehumanized, demonized, but as fellow human beings deserving respect for their personhood and dignity, that we will conduct a discourse that just might prevent conflict. There is room for everyone; there is room for every culture, race, language, and point of view.

Chapter 6

All, All Are God's Children

On Including Gays and Lesbians in the Church and Society

Desmond Tutu dissents from the official policies of most of the world's Anglican churches, which hold that gays and lesbians should be celibate; and in the years since his retirement as archbishop of Cape Town he has become one of the world's most prominent figures pleading for a change in the attitudes of religious institutions toward human sexuality.

1

Tutu's position is reflected in excerpts from a newspaper article and a sermon preached in Southwark Cathedral, London, in 2004.

A student once asked me, If I could have one wish granted to reverse an injustice, what would it be? I had to ask for two. One is for world leaders to forgive the debts of developing nations which hold them in such thrall. The other is for the world to end the persecution of people because of their sexual orientation, which is every bit as unjust as that crime against humanity, apartheid.

This is a matter of ordinary justice. We struggled against apartheid in South Africa, supported by people the world over, because black people were being blamed and made to suffer for something we could do nothing about—our very skin. It is the same with sexual orientation. It is a given. I could not have fought against the discrimination of apartheid and not also fight against the discrimination that homosexuals endure, even in our churches and faith groups.

I am proud that in South Africa, when we won the chance to build our own new constitution, the human rights of all have been explicitly enshrined in our laws. My hope is that one day this will be the case all over the world, and that *all* will have equal rights. For me this struggle is a seamless robe. Opposing apartheid was a matter of justice. Opposing discrimination against women is a matter of justice. Opposing discrimination on the basis of sexual orientation is a matter of justice.

It is also a matter of love. Every human being is precious. We are all—*all* of us—part of God's family. We all must be allowed to love each other with honor. Yet all over the world, lesbian, gay, bisexual, and transgender people are persecuted. We treat them as pariahs and push them outside our communities. We make them doubt that they too are children of God. This must be nearly the ultimate blasphemy. We blame them for what they are.

Churches say that the expression of love in a heterosexual monogamous relationship includes the physical—the touching, embracing, kissing, the genital act; the totality of our love makes each of us grow to become increasingly godlike and compassionate. If this is so for the heterosexual, what earthly reasons have we to say that it is not the case with the homosexual?

The Jesus I worship is not likely to collaborate with those who vilify and persecute an already oppressed minority. I myself could not have opposed the injustice of penalizing people for something about which they could do nothing—their race—and then have kept quiet as women were being penalized for something they could do nothing about—their gender; hence my support for the ordination of women to the priesthood and the episcopate.

Equally, I cannot keep quiet while people are being penalized for something about which they can do nothing—their sexuality. To discriminate against our sisters and brothers who are lesbian or gay on grounds of their sexual orientation for me is as totally unacceptable and unjust as apartheid ever was.

2

Tutu's most characteristic pulpit appeals for inclusiveness are reflected in excerpts from sermons preached in St. Paul's Cathedral, London, Ontario, and All Saints' Church, Pasadena, California.

You and I are meant to say that there is an openness demonstrated by the arms of our Lord strung out on the cross as if to embrace the whole cosmos, because it was God's intention to include, to bring all things to a unity, in our Lord and Savior Jesus Christ. There is nothing that must be left outside. God's writ runs everywhere, and you and I have often been too adept at trying to discover who may come in and who may be excluded.

God has no enemies, ultimately, for all, all—the atheist, the sinner, every one of those whom we have tended in our respectabilities to push outside—are God's children. Our concern must be to find out how we embrace everybody, how we bring everybody inside, how we say, "We are all equal, of equal worth in the sight of our Father."

Jesus did not say, "I, if I be lifted up, I will draw some." Jesus said, "I, if I be lifted up from the earth, I will draw all, all, all, all, all" (John 12:32, KJV)—black, white, yellow, rich, poor, clever, not so clever, beautiful, not so beautiful. It's one of the most radical things. All, all, all belong: gay, lesbian, so-called straight. All, all are meant to be held in this incredible embrace that will not let us go. All.

PART TWO

International Campaigner
for Justice

CHAPTER 7

Freedom Is Cheaper Than Repression

On Democracy in Africa

The award to Desmond Tutu of the Nobel Peace Prize in 1984 magnified his voice internationally beyond the church and anti-apartheid circles in which he had moved until then. One of the first organizations to take advantage of his new stature was the All Africa Conference of Churches (AACC), the ecumenical council representing the Protestant churches of Africa, which elected Tutu as its president in 1987. Tutu knew the churches and nations of Africa better than most: working for the Theological Education Fund in the early 1970s, he visited seminaries, universities, and churches in situations as widely varied as Nigeria recovering from civil war, Uganda under the dictatorship of Idi Amin, Rwanda and Burundi after tens of thousands had died in intergroup conflict, Angola and Mozambique under Portuguese rule, and Zimbabwe while it was still ruled by whites as Rhodesia. His early experiences in Africa helped equip him to speak with confidence to what he saw as the failings of the new democratic South African government after liberation; his trip notes from the 1970s show that he saw very little in South Africa after 1994 which he had not seen two decades earlier in one or another newly free African nation.[1] As president of the AACC, Tutu drew on his anti-apartheid credentials, his knowledge of Africa, and his stature as Nobel Peace laureate to support the continent's churches as they campaigned for human rights in what has been called Africa's "second wave" of liberation, during which multiparty democracy mushroomed across the continent after the end of the Cold War.

1

Tutu first outlined the approach he was to take in an address to the AACC general assembly that elected him president. The assembly's theme was "You Shall Be My Witnesses," drawn from Jesus's exhortation to his apostles, as recorded in Acts 1:8.

We are true witnesses if we are on the side of the weak, the powerless, the exploited, if we have solidarity with them; if we care for the widow, the orphan, and the stranger; if we are the servants of God. But when we side with the poor and the weak and the unimportant ones as the world computes importance, then the powerful ones don't like it, then the privileged ones resent it, and you will suffer and maybe you will die.

Jesus said, "Unless you take up your cross and follow me, you can't be my disciple" (Luke 14:27). A church that does not suffer can't be the church of Jesus Christ. If you speak up as Archbishop Janani Luwum in Uganda did,[2] and as others have done and are doing in many parts of the continent, you may be killed. But Jesus said, "Unless a grain of wheat falls into the earth and dies, it remains alone; but if it dies, it bears much fruit" (John 12:24, RSV).

The voiceless, the weak, the oppressed, the exploited have no one to champion them except the church. We must be patriots who love our countries and nations passionately as the prophets of Israel loved their country, their land, and their people. Our love should inspire us to want only the best for our nations, to be involved in true development so that people can enter into the fullness of all that God has intended for them, that they may begin to enjoy life—because Christ said, "I have come that they may have life, and life in its abundance" (John 10:10), in its effervescent abundance.

We must be custodians of the human rights of those who have their human rights outraged. We will say, "Let them become subjects, not objects. Let them be able to participate as those who take control over their future." We pray, "Please, God, help the countries in Africa to become successful in their independence." Because, my friends, when there is a coup, when there is a military takeover in this, that, or the other country, you set back the liberation struggle in South Africa: the racists in South Africa say, "Aha, we told you they couldn't do it."

We must love our nations and our countries, but that can't be through the corruption, injustice, and oppression of the powerful, the rich. It pains us to have to admit that there is less freedom and personal liberty in most of independent Africa than there was during the much-maligned colonial days. The gospel of Jesus Christ cannot allow us to keep silent in the face of this. The truth of the gospel constrains us to speak up and to speak out against that which is contrary to it.

I believe that the church in Africa must be committed to liberation. Our God is the great liberator, the God of the Exodus, leading a rabble of slaves out of bondage to set them free from all that makes them less than what God intends them to be, setting them free to be his people. We must be committed to the total liberation of God's children, politically, socially, economically, so they can enjoy what Paul calls the glorious liberty of the children of God. This is most obviously so for your sisters and brothers in South Africa, but it would be true too for many in independent Africa for whom all that seems to have changed is the complexion of the oppressor as the rich have grown richer and the poor have become poorer. They wait for us to witness for God by speaking up for them.

2

Over the ensuing decade, Tutu used his AACC presidential visits to secure access to heads of state across Africa and to encourage member churches to lobby for democracy. In February 1989 he traveled to Angola—ruled by a government that claimed to be Marxist-Leninist—and Zaire—ruled by the notoriously corrupt

*pro-Western dictator Mobutu Sese Seko. In the Angolan capital,
Luanda, he preached to twenty thousand Angolans in a basketball
stadium.*

We live in a beautiful continent, but it is a continent that is
bleeding. It is a continent that has suffered. It is a continent
that has been exploited during the period of colonialism. It is a
continent many of whose people were captured to be made slaves.
It is a continent at the present time where there is a great deal of
suffering. It is a continent that is being destroyed by civil war. It is
suffering in places such as Ethiopia, the Sudan, and Mozambique.
It suffers in Angola because of the civil war and the struggle against
the injustice and oppression of apartheid.

It is a continent that suffers because it has to bear such a heavy
burden of international debt. It is a continent that suffers from
malnutrition. It is a continent that suffers from poverty. It is a continent that suffers from gross exploitation by those who are rich. It
is a continent where there is very little justice, and we know that in
our part of the world there is suffering because God's children are
treated as if they were dirt because of the color of their skin.

And so we sometimes ask, Where are you, God, in the suffering
of Africa? God, do you love black people like you love other people?
God, why must we bear so much suffering because of the color of
our skin? Why must we be thrown into a fiery furnace of suffering
and pain and exploitation?

Then we remember that we have a God who does not give us
advice, who does not write us letters to tell us how to solve our

problems; we don't have a God who stands miles and miles away from us. Our God comes, our God enters the furnace of our suffering, for our God is Emmanuel. Our God came in our Lord and Savior Jesus Christ to set us free from all that makes us less than what God wants us to be. Jesus Christ died on the cross to make us free, to make us the sons and the daughters of God. Jesus Christ came so that we should know that each one of us is special to God, that each one of us is a child of God.

My friends, I stand before you to assure you that God is with you, that your struggle for true independence in this land will succeed, that our struggle in South Africa and in Namibia will succeed, that we will all be free together, and we will all be one family together; for "if God be for us, who can be against us?" (Romans 8:31, KJV).

3

In Zaire (which would be renamed the Democratic Republic of the Congo after Mobutu's overthrow in 1997), theological students responded with as much enthusiasm to Tutu's remarks on oppression and the Bible as did young people in South Africa at the time. These remarks were made against the background of tension between students and Mobutu's government.

In many countries that are totalitarian or oppressive, the governments have certain literature which they ban. In South Africa many books are prohibited. We say to the government of South Africa, "You are too late, because the book you should have banned long ago is the Bible, for that is the most revolutionary book in a situation of oppression."

St. Paul says each one of us is a temple of the Holy Spirit. To treat one such person as if they were less than this is not just wrong, it is blasphemous, and we don't get this from a political manifesto. We get it from the Bible. And we learn from the Bible that God is a God who takes sides. He is not neutral. God is a God who is always on the side of the poor, the oppressed, the little ones who are despised; and it is for that reason that we, his church, have got to be in solidarity with the poor, the homeless, the hungry, and the oppressed.

So, my brothers and sisters, you are called to a high calling. You are to remind the church that whenever it is obedient to this Lord and Master, the church will end up, as its Lord and Master did, on the cross. Because when the church speaks up on behalf of the weak and the poor, the powerful and the rich don't like it and the church must suffer. A church that does not suffer is not the church of Jesus Christ.

4

The main Sunday service of the Zaire visit was moved by the government from a stadium in Kinshasa to the fenced grounds of the

national legislature, the Palais du Peuple, which was more easily
controlled by Mobutu's troops.

Africa has the unenviable distinction of producing the world's greatest number of refugees. Of course, many of these are refugees from natural disasters. But sadly, my brothers and sisters, the majority of these refugees are refugees from injustice and oppression in their motherlands. For we must confess, sadly and humbly, that Africa has one of the worst records of violations of human rights. Africa has a spate of military dictatorships.

In many places, all that has changed for the people who suffer is the complexion of the oppressor. In colonial times the oppressor was of a different complexion. Sadly, today the complexion of the oppressor is the same as the complexion of the oppressed.

So we say to all unjust rulers everywhere: "Beware! Watch it! Look out in South Africa. Look out wherever you may be, unjust ruler." We have no doubt that we shall be free. The blood of Jesus Christ bought us so that we would be free to enjoy the glorious liberty of the children of God.

5

In October 1989, Tutu visited Khartoum, Sudan, four months after
Omar Hassan al-Bashir (who was still ruling the country when this
book went to press) had seized control of the government in a military
coup. As in Kinshasa, Tutu's most pointed strictures were not osten-
sibly directed at the government of his hosts. But also as in Kinshasa,

students at Khartoum University drew their own parallels, as shown by their applause when he cited abuses which were common to both South Africa and Sudan.

Friends, Africa has many gifts that it can give to the world, but Africa is in agony, Africa is in anguish; Africa is suffering from poverty, from malnutrition, from all sorts of ghastly things. Africa also suffers from one of the most horrendous human rights records. And it has got nothing to do with politics to say that we cannot afford this situation. We cannot have people say it is bad to have detention without trial in South Africa, and they quite rightly condemn it, and then when it happens elsewhere they expect you to keep quiet. You have to say if it is wrong there, it must be wrong everywhere else where it happens. Africa, if we're not careful, will die. And we will be answerable before the judgment seat of God. What did you do? What did you do to stand up for justice?

We have to say we are deeply, deeply distressed at what is happening here, this civil war, where children die of starvation, where so many are displaced. We can't pretend it is not happening, friends. The Muslim greeting is "Salaam." Salaam is peace—peace not in the negative sense, but peace meaning you strive for prosperity, for wholeness, for goodness, for compassion, for love, for caring, for sharing. If you do not, then you are not a good Muslim. If you do not strive for the establishment of the kingdom of God, if you are a Christian or Jew, you are not a good Christian, not a good Jew.

We come humbly, we come trembling, but to say, brothers and sisters, if you fail here, you make us fail down there in South Africa. Because they always say to us, "You say you want freedom, black people, but what do you know about freedom? Look at what they are doing in Ethiopia, look at what they are doing in the Sudan, look at what they are doing in Uganda," and then we sit and suffer under apartheid. You see, we belong together. If you succeed, we succeed; if you fail, we fail. And so we pray that you will exert yourselves, and we will do all we can to participate with you, so that one day Africa will be truly free—*all* of Africa, black and white and yellow and green and all of God's children.

6

From Khartoum, Tutu went to Addis Ababa, where Mengistu Haile Mariam presided over the totalitarian regime he had established after deposing Haile Selassie, Ethiopia's traditional ruler, fifteen years earlier. When the sermon from which the following excerpts were taken was preached in Addis Ababa, there was a stir among members of the congregation who spoke both English and Amharic, the language into which it was being translated. They afterward explained that the sermon translated was not the same as that preached—such things were not said in public in Amharic in Ethiopia.

Do you remember the story of the prophet Elijah, when he had a competition with four hundred prophets of Baal (1 Kings 18:17–39)? He said to the children of Israel, "You must choose between God and Baal, the false god." He said, "We are going to have a competition; we must choose two bulls. You, the prophets of Baal, must slaughter your bull, place it on the firewood, but do not light the fire. I will take the other bull; I will slaughter it and I will place it on the firewood and I will also not light the fire. Then each group must call on his god, and the god who answers with fire, that is the real God." So Elijah said to the prophets of Baal, "You start first: call on your god." And the prophets of Baal danced, and they called to their god, "Baal, please hear us!" They danced, they cut themselves, they did all sorts of things, calling out, "Baal, please hear us!" But nothing happened. And Elijah was lying on the ground there and really laughing at the prophets of Baal. He said to them, "Shout louder. Maybe your god is deaf; he can't hear. Maybe he is on holiday. Maybe your god is asleep. Maybe he has just gone"—well, in the Bible it says maybe he has gone to the other side to relieve himself.

The point is: our God never takes a day off. Our God is always there. Our God does not take a holiday. Our God is not deaf. Our God is never asleep. Do you remember when God spoke to Moses? He said, "I have seen the suffering of my people. I have heard their cry. I know their suffering and am come down to deliver them." When we were enslaved by the devil, God saw our suffering as a result of our slavery to the devil. God knew, God saw, and God came down in our Lord and Savior Jesus Christ to deliver us from our bondage.

You look around Africa at this time, at God's children suffering all over Africa—the poor getting poorer, the hungry getting hungrier. You look over all of Africa and you see many of God's children suffering oppression. You see God's children many times in prison for nothing. All over Africa you see God's children treated as if they were rubbish. In many parts of Africa you see God's children having their noses rubbed in the dust. You see God's children trodden underfoot by the powerful. In many parts of Africa God's children can't speak what they want to say because when they say, "No, this is wrong," they are taken to prison or they are killed. Not just in South Africa, although there it is most obvious.

But look at all of Africa. There are wars here, there, everywhere. The wars in the Sudan, in Chad, in Ethiopia. And people ask, "Where is God? Where is God when we suffer in this way?" We come to tell you that our God is a God who sees. Our God is a God who knows. Our God is a God who hears. As God's children cry because of their bondage, as they cry because of their starvation and their hunger, God knows, God sees, God hears, and God comes down to deliver his children. God comes to deliver his children from their bondage, because God is a God who sides with the hungry and the poor and the marginalized.

So we are able to tell the powerful everywhere, we tell the oppressor everywhere, "Watch it! Watch it! Watch it! Because God comes to deliver." If you are an oppressor, then you are opposed to God, and who are you to try to stand up against God; and so we tell the children of God everywhere that God will make you free. God calls on all of you who are the followers of his Son to be those who work together with God, to be those who feed the hungry on behalf of God, to be those who clothe the naked on behalf of God, to give water to the thirsty on behalf of God. God calls on you who are his fellow workers, his partners, to work for justice and peace, so that Africa, so that Ethiopia, so that *every* land will be a land that recognizes God as Lord and King.

Nineteen months later, Mengistu's regime collapsed under the combined pressure of rebels from the Tigray Province, an independence war by Eritreans, and the withdrawal of Soviet support after Mikhail Gorbachev came to power. As Tigrayan and Eritrean forces closed in on Addis Ababa, Mengistu fled into exile in Zimbabwe. He was tried in absentia on charges of genocide as defined in Ethiopian law. He was convicted and sentenced to life imprisonment; an appeals court later overturned the sentence and imposed the death penalty. In 2010 Zimbabwean President Robert Mugabe was still giving him asylum.

7

In 1990 Tutu spread his campaign for respect for human rights in Africa to West Africa, where on visits to Ghana and Nigeria he propagated a slogan—which he had first used in Kenya—about the costs of authoritarian rule.

We keep trying to say to rulers, in Africa and everywhere, who are not democratic rulers, "Hey, just learn one little truth: freedom is cheaper than repression!" Because when you are a popular leader, when you are a leader chosen by the people, you don't need too much security; all the people are your security guards.

Please, please, please, rulers in Africa, give the people the freedom to choose and to choose freely. Once you do that, once you open up and say to the people, "You are free," the energies that they release are incredible, because the people have a remarkable pride, a deep patriotism. They want to see their country succeed so that they can walk tall, walk proud, and can say, "I come from Ghana and we are free in Ghana," "I come from Nigeria and we are free; we can say anything we like."

Almost everywhere, the rulers are out of touch with their people. They dare not go among their people. Africa is too precious to be left in the hands of dictators. People have forgotten the African way of ruling. Almost everywhere in Africa the good chief was the man who could listen and then draw a consensus. Consensus happens because people have their different points of view and the good ruler says, "I have listened to all of you; we are not taking a vote, but listening to you I think most of you are feeling that we must go this way rather than that way."

Now the ruler who could discern what the people wanted was the ruler who lasted on his throne. The ruler who didn't somehow didn't last so long. We would like our rulers to last because they are rulers by the will and consent of the people. We want Africa to be the star of the world because it is a continent that is richly, richly endowed and has been impoverished by rulers who have far too frequently enriched themselves at the cost of the ordinary people.

So we say, "Viva freedom! Long live freedom! Long live democracy! Long live the people!"

CHAPTER 8

Watch It! Watch It!

On Hope and Human Rights in Situations of Conflict

Beyond Africa, Desmond Tutu was invited in 1989 to join the heads of the Anglican churches in Canada (Archbishop Michael Peers), the United States (Presiding Bishop Edmond Browning), and the West Indies (Archbishop Orland Lindsay) in a pastoral visit to Central America. Two years later he visited Ireland.

1

In Nicaragua the Sandinista government was in power, and the U.S. administration was supporting the Contra rebels who were trying to overthrow it. In a sermon in St. Francis Church, Managua, Tutu gave the Nicaraguans the same message he preached to those who suffered in Africa.

We have come to say to you, our sisters and brothers in Nicaragua, that you are not alone. You have sisters and brothers more than you can number in so many parts of the world. We want to share a few words with you, for we have been strengthened by your witness.

Do you remember the wonderful biblical story of those three young men (Daniel 3)? The king set up a huge statue and he said, "Everyone in this land must worship this statue. Anyone who refuses to worship the statue of the king is going to be put into a fiery furnace." You remember those three young men who said, "We will not worship the statue of the king." The king got very angry, really angry, and said, "What! You won't worship my statue?" They said, "Yes, king." And the king said, "Hey, make that furnace seven times hotter than it has been before." And the three young men said, "Well, we have a God. We worship this God. This is the true God. We hope, of course, that he will deliver us. But even if he does not deliver us, we will still worship him." The furnace was so hot that we are told the people who were carrying the three into the furnace were burned to cinders. Well, I mean, it's a story, so I don't know how they threw them in, but they threw them in. And then the king looked and he saw something that surprised him. They were not burned to death. He looked and he saw the three young men. They were walking in the fire! No, no! They were not three. There was a fourth with them. The king looked and he said, "There is a fourth who looks like a god."

That is the God we worship. We worship a God who does not

give good advice from a great, safe distance away. Our God is a God who enters the furnace of tribulation with us. Our God is Emmanuel—"God with us." Now we come to Nicaragua. And we hear all the history of the suffering of the people of Nicaragua under the dictatorship of Somoza;[1] how people used to disappear, how people used to be arrested, how the rich got richer and the poor got poorer. The people called out to God and said, "We are in a furnace here." God came and God was with the people of Nicaragua, and God set free the people of Nicaragua. Everybody said, "Ah, heaven has come to earth." And then the war broke out. Some of the rich of the world decided they wanted to teach Nicaragua a lesson.[2] We come again, and we find the people of Nicaragua suffering. The people of Nicaragua want peace, but they cannot get peace. The people of Nicaragua want to be able to live in harmony. And so the people wonder, Where is God?

We've come to say to you, Our God, your God, is not far away somewhere in heaven. Our God, your God, is here. Your God, our God, is the fourth in the furnace of fire. Our God, your God, decided to come as a human baby. Your God, our God, was born in a stable. Your God, our God, said, *says,* "I love you. I love you as if you were the only human being on earth. I love you so much that I am ready to give you the best that I have. Not this, not that. I give you my only begotten Son. I love you with a love that does not change. I love you with a love that is forever. I love you, and so I hang on the cross for you. You matter to me. You, you, and you: I know you by name." Isn't that wonderful? The very hairs of your head are numbered. Our Lord Jesus Christ says you are of more value than the sparrows. And yet, not one sparrow falls to the ground without your Father knowing.

Jesus says, "When I was hungry, you fed me. When I was naked, you clothed me. When I was thirsty, you gave me to drink. When I was in prison, you visited me" (Matthew 25:35–36). And you say, "Uh, uh! When did we see you when you were in this condition?" Then Jesus says, "Inasmuch as you have done it to the least of these, my sisters and my brothers, you have done it to me" (v. 40). Do you want to know who is God? Well, turn to your right and turn to your left. There you have your God.

We have a wonderful God. For our God says each one of us is of so great a value that we are God-carriers. Each one of us. St. Paul says we are sanctuaries of the Holy Spirit. We are temples of God, each one of us—each one of us here, every one of us. God says, "I am with you in the most intimate kind of way. And you especially who are poor, you especially who are downtrodden. I, your God, care particularly for those—those who are without a voice in the world, those who are treated as if they were nothing." Those are God's special concern, those who are in the furnace of suffering and anguish. Those know that we have a God who enters the furnace. We have a God, the almighty God, who is also the weak God. We have a wonderful God, the eternal, immortal one, but he is a dying God. For our God enters our situation. Our God identifies with us. So we share with you here in Nicaragua and say that actually, when you suffer, in some ways God is saying, "You are special to me." Just look at what God did to

God's Son. When you are God's favorite, God leaves you to hang on a cross.

God asks us, "Will you please help me? Will you please help me save the world?" God comes to the people of Nicaragua and says, "In and through your suffering, in and through the cross that you bear, please help me, help me to save the world." Offer your suffering so that God can transfigure the ugliness of this world. God is asking you here, "Please be my partners. Will you please be my collaborators? Will you please help me to change the ugliness of the world? Will you please help me to bring peace where there is war? Will you please help me to bring reconciliation where there is quarrelling? Will you please help me to bring joy where there is sadness? Will you please help me to bring togetherness where there is separation? Will you please help me to collect and bring together those who are separated? Will you please help me to make my children know that they are my children, that we belong together, that we will survive only together, that we will be free only together, that we will be human only together?"

And so know, dear sisters and brothers, that our God is with you, our God is Emmanuel. Our God has entered the furnace with you. And our God is the God of the Exodus. Our God is the liberator God. Our God is leading you out of your bondage. Our God leads you into the Promised Land.

2

From Nicaragua the archbishops traveled to Panama, where the de facto ruler was the military dictator General Manuel Noriega. The country was tense in the run-up to an election in May, which had been called against a backdrop of political detentions and restrictions on press freedom. The visiting church leaders agreed to see Noriega only after resolving to state publicly afterward that they had questioned him on his regime's attitude toward human rights. Tutu's barely concealed allusions to Noriega's oppressive rule under cover of remarks about apartheid South Africa were met with laughter and whoops of delight when he addressed an audience in the civic center of Panama City during Holy Week.

Those who oppose the government of South Africa, those who oppose its injustice and its oppression, are dealt with very severely. Sometimes they are banished from their homes in a kind of internal exile. Sometimes they are banned, which means they are restricted, like being put under house arrest. Sometimes they are detained without trial. I am wearing a red ribbon here tonight. The churches in our country have asked us to wear red ribbons in solidarity with people in detention without trial. Some have been in detention without trial for as long as three years. They have never been brought to court. They have not been found guilty of any crime. The police decide you are a security risk and you disappear, and your family members don't know where you go. They often may not be able to visit you. Sometimes people get assassinated because they are opponents of the government, and the police somehow are unable to find their murderers. It is a very strange coincidence—the enemies of apartheid can be killed and the police are not able to find who killed them. The headquarters of the opponents of apartheid are firebombed or petrol-bombed. Nobody seems to be able to find the culprits. To oppose apartheid becomes increasingly criminalized: some who have opposed apartheid have been found guilty of treason.

Television and the radio in South Africa are state propaganda instruments. The opponents of the government are vilified on television and over the radio, and they don't get a chance to reply. The press is severely restricted. Some newspapers are closed— I'm talking about South Africa.

Often and often our people are filled with despair, and they wonder, What have we done to deserve all this suffering? It is important for the church of God to tell the people of God, "Hey, hey, hey! Our God sees. Our God hears. Our God knows, and our God will come down and deliver us." And we say it. We say it—in South Africa—we say to them, "Hey! Hey! Hey! We are going to be free. We are not asking for permission from the rulers of our land. We *know* we are going to be free." And we say to our oppressors, "Do you know what? We are being nice to you. We are inviting you to join the winning side. Come and join the winning side because you have already lost."

Because this is what the Bible says about the good ruler: "God, give your own justice to the king, your own righteousness to the Royal Son." Why? "So that he may rule your people rightly and your people with justice, that he will defend the poorest, he will save the children of those in need. The good ruler will crush the oppressors. The good ruler will free the poor man who calls to him and those who need help. He will have pity on the poor and the feeble and save the lives of those in need" (Psalm 72).

I'm reading from the Bible. I am not reading from the manifesto of a political party. The good ruler will redeem the lives of the needy from exploitation and outrage because their lives are precious in his sight. If you are a ruler and you are not this kind of ruler, you are in trouble. You are in real trouble with God. You are in very real trouble. We try to tell oppressors everywhere, "You are not God. You are just an ordinary human being. Maybe you have got a lot of power now. Ah, ah, but watch it! Watch it! Watch it!"

You know, Hitler thought he had a lot of power. Where is Hitler today? Mussolini thought he had a lot of power. Where is he today? Franco thought he had a lot of power. Somoza . . . Uh, I'm going to Africa. I must cross the sea and go to Africa. Idi Amin thought he had a lot of power. Where is he today? We could go on and on like that. And we say, "This is God's world, and God is in charge in his world."

Therefore, we can stand upright with our heads held high. We don't apologize for our existence. God did not make a mistake in creating us. Our God hears. Our God cares. Our God knows and our God will come down to deliver his people. Our God will come to deliver his people here, everywhere, in South Africa, today—maybe not today. Tomorrow? Maybe not tomorrow. But what can separate us from the love of God? Absolutely nothing can separate us from the love of God in our Lord and Savior Jesus Christ.

Noriega's favored candidate lost the May 1989 elections, so he declared the results void. After a standoff with the United States— which still had military bases in Panama—Noriega was overthrown by U.S. military forces in December 1989. Later jailed in Florida for drug trafficking, racketeering, and money laundering, he was extradited to France in 2010 to face money-laundering charges there.

3

In Ireland, Tutu's outspokenness on talks about the North's future created alarm in 1991. At the time, the British were trying to convene new all-party talks on Northern Ireland but were excluding the republicans represented by Sinn Féin, on the grounds of the Irish Republican Army's use of violence. Tutu addressed the issue in the course of a sermon preached at a televised service in Dublin's Christ Church Cathedral.

Friends, we pray for you in this beautiful island home. We offer our sympathies to those who have suffered on both sides in the troubles that have beset this island. We give thanks to God for those, in the churches and elsewhere, working for reconciliation and peace and tolerance, who call for a celebration of the rich diversity of cultural and religious and political perspectives and traditions.

We condemn all violence, from whatever quarter, and call on those who perpetrate it to give peace and negotiations a chance. I have no right or special expertise to speak to you of your complex problems and difficulties, except that I come out of a crucible of like suffering; and as your feeble brother, I say, Let your negotiations be as inclusive as possible. Don't let any feel they have been left out.

Any group, however small, which has grievances, real or imaginary, must not feel excluded; otherwise you can kiss goodbye to peace. Let them be represented by those they regard as their authentic spokespersons; otherwise talks, as we have discovered at home, become an exercise in futility. Take heart, for people who swore that they would never speak to each other are now engaged in talks in South Africa. It can happen here too.

After the service a journalist asked whether the sermon had been calling for Sinn Féin's inclusion.

I have said the talks should be inclusive, and people have got to decide for themselves here what that means—I mean, who are the groups who are representative of constituencies. We don't come with prescriptions.

A senior British diplomat responded to the sermon by intercepting Tutu in a cathedral corridor and pleading with him not to upset delicate negotiations that were taking place behind the scenes.

4

In an interview with the BBC in Northern Ireland, Tutu alluded to the violence caused during South Africa's transition over the fear of Chief Mangosuthu Buthelezi's Inkatha Freedom Party that it would be sidelined in talks between the African National Congress and the apartheid government.

I am speaking out of our own experience at home. Whenever any group has thought that it was going to be marginalized, then we could just as well say there was no hope of talks succeeding. One is just saying that if we are concerned for peace and reconciliation—as I'm sure you are in Northern Ireland—then however small the group, if it feels it has grievances and is excluded, then there is no chance of that group being able to accept whatever agreements are reached.

If people are concerned about violence and so on, we have experiences at home, where in the case of Namibia they were able to say, "We speak to the internal wing of Swapo, which is not involved in violence or the armed struggle, and we are not going to speak to the group that is involved in violence." But I do not want to be prescribing to you.

When you put many preconditions, that makes the talks more vulnerable: the other side may then want to put its set of conditions. We want to pray that the movement toward negotiation be as uncluttered as possible and to remove as many preconditions as possible. I am not saying you shouldn't have any preconditions at all—but the fewer preconditions, the greater the chance that you are going to be able to include everybody and the greater the chance that the conclusions that you arrive at through those talks will be acceptable to most parties.

Most people want peace, and I have no doubt at all that you will come out successful at the end.

Later, the British government established secret contacts with the IRA as part of the peace process that led to the Good Friday Agreement of 1998.

CHAPTER 9

Our Salvation Is of the Jews

On the Israeli-Palestinian Conflict

Desmond Tutu's views on the Middle East have triggered the most virulent criticism of him since the attacks he faced from white South Africans in the 1980s—criticism that has been sustained over two decades. First focusing on the military collaboration between South Africa's apartheid government and Israel in the 1970s, Tutu began after he won the Nobel Peace Prize to extend his comments to cover relations between Israelis and Palestinians.

1

Tutu's first intervention in this arena was made at the Stephen Wise Free Synagogue in New York City in January 1989. Much of his address acknowledged the Jewish roots of the Christian faith and sketched the Old Testament demands for justice. The part that gave rise to the most debate is included here.

You have been a tremendous light to the world, and we who are the oppressed of today give great thanks to God for yourselves. We are proud to acknowledge the riches of our Jewish heritage. We are proud to acknowledge that we too are the descendants of Abraham. We give thanks to God for the Jewish people. I do not say this here because I am in this place. It is just part of our tradition. Your history is our history. God seems to work in extraordinary ways. At home, many of those in the forefront of the struggle have been Jews, and we salute them. I remember with great thankfulness that, when we were being investigated by the South African government and I was general secretary of the South African Council of Churches, our chief counsel was Sydney Kentridge[1] of the Biko inquest fame, an extraordinary person.

We thank God that Israel as a nation has come into being. That nation has a right to territorial integrity and fundamental security against attacks from those who deny her right to exist. I condemn categorically all forms of terrorism from whatever source, wherever—in this particular case, terrorism against Israel; though Israelis must remember that in their fight for independence some of their leaders engaged in what the world would have described as terrorism. But Israel as a nation and Jews as individuals are not infallible, mercifully. They could not want to claim to be God. That would be idolatry and unforgivable. However, often and often, when Israel as a government or as a nation is criticized for some aspect of her policy, too many Jews are too quick to accuse critics of being anti-Semitic. I have fallen foul of many Jews because of this ploy. It is wonderful to know there are Jews within Israel who remember the high standards of justice and conduct that are expected of Israel. And so you could have half a million Jews protest Israel's involvement in the horrors of the Lebanese refugee camps a few years ago. Those protestors did Israel proud, and have shown that as a country it is fundamentally democratic. It is not afraid of self-criticism.

Blacks in South Africa and in this country, I believe, and oppressed people everywhere have assumed that Jews as a matter of course would side with them against injustice, exploitation, and oppression, given the nature of your history as a saga of survival against all of this. Therefore, I have to say yet again: we blacks in South Africa cannot understand how people with your kind of history could allow the government of Israel, as distinct from the people, to have the kind of relationship with the government of South Africa that it has, to be involved in cooperation with that government on nuclear matters, and especially on security matters, providing, we believe, the South African government with techniques for suppressing uprisings. We cannot understand how Jews can cooperate with a government many of whose members were sympathetic to Hitler and the Nazis and who for a long time refused Jews membership in their political party because they were Jews. Of course, I find it bizarre that a Jew would want to become a member of the Nationalist Party now that that is possible, but that is another matter. To criticize Israel for this collaboration with the Nationalists who are carrying out a policy against blacks akin to Nazism is not to be anti-Semitic. Whether Jews so accuse me or not, I will continue to be highly critical of Israel in this regard.

Black and Jewish relations in South Africa and in the United States will suffer grievously until Israel repudiates categorically that policy and distances itself conspicuously from the South African government. When that happens, there will be a dramatic improvement in relations.

Not that they will become completely amicable, because there is yet another obstacle, and that is the question of the Palestinians. I have not spoken on this issue in public before tonight because of apprehension that I would be called anti-Semitic. I have to say I find it very, very difficult to understand Israel's policy in this regard. I do not know all the factors that are involved. My position is made more difficult because of two factors. I am a Christian, and many of the Palestinians are Christians—in fact, many are Anglicans—and their anguish tears my heart apart. Second, it is because I am a black South African, and if you changed the names, the description of what is happening in the Gaza Strip and the West Bank could be a description of what is happening in South Africa. It is uncanny and it is deeply, deeply distressing. Israel cannot do that: it is out of line with her biblical and historical traditions. Israel, or shall we say the Jews, having suffered so much, cannot allow their government to cause other people to suffer so much. Jews, having been dispossessed for so long, cannot allow their government to dispossess others. Jews, having been victims of gross injustice, cannot allow their government to make others victims of injustice. It is such a horrific contradiction. Sadly but truly, until the Palestinian question is settled equitably, relations with blacks in South Africa and I believe in the United States will not improve significantly.

Now I want to make a suggestion. It is a suggestion that I am making for the first time here. I am making it without having consulted Eli Wiesel. He and I are Nobel Peace laureates. Might it not be possible that he and I jointly be mediators in this matter? I offer myself humbly but as one committed to justice, reconciliation, and peace. Second, I ask that you, powerful as you are in the United States, must press Israel hard on the matter of a just settlement for the Palestinians. I ask that you press Israel hard to repudiate its policy on South Africa. I ask that you press the United States administration hard on civil rights issues relating to blacks and other minorities. I ask that you make it quite clear that you will not support any U.S. administration, Democrat or Republican, that collaborates with the South African government. I ask that you help put pressure on the American government to put pressure on the South African government to do at least these things: lift the state of emergency, release all political prisoners and detainees, unban our political organizations, and negotiate a new constitution for a democratic, just, and nonracial South Africa. I ask that you pressure the banks in this land as the rolling-over of bank loans for the South African government comes up for review, that the banks must not let that rollover happen until, at the very least, the things that I have just enumerated are on the agenda.

I ask finally: please join us in a campaign. To oppose apartheid nonviolently is becoming increasingly difficult. Nonviolent opposition to apartheid is being criminalized, to the extent that when you oppose apartheid, you are found guilty of treason. There are some outstanding black leaders who have been found guilty of treason in

the so-called Delmas trial.[2] I plead that you will help us to insist
that they have an early appeal against this horrendous judgment
and that they be out on bail when the appeal is being heard. All of
this, my friends, comes from the heart. It is a *cri de coeur*. Salvation,
our salvation, is of the Jews.[3]

2

*Tutu's Christmas pilgrimage to the Holy Land in 1989 was made
with Michael Nuttall, bishop of Natal and the newly elected dean
of the Anglican Church in Southern Africa, and Njongonkulu
Ndungane, the church's executive officer and later Tutu's successor as
archbishop. Accompanied by their host, the Anglican bishop of Jerusalem, Samir Kafity, the party visited Muslim, Jewish, and Christian
holy places. Tutu spoke to journalists near the Islamic shrine known
as the Dome of the Rock.*

We support the struggle of the Palestinian people in their
longing for statehood and independence. We are struggling
for our own self-determination in South Africa.

We support the Jewish people in their right to exist as an independent nation.

We pray for the day to come soon when the Palestinian state will
exist side by side with the Jewish state, and Arab and Jew will hold
hands together as those who say "Shalom" and "Salaam."

3

At Jerusalem's Western Wall, he gave an extemporaneous message to Jewish religious officials.

Our faith is one that has its roots in Judaism, which says that justice is the basis of faith and also the basis of peace. In Jerusalem, the city of peace, we pray that he whom we Christians call the Prince of Peace will bless all the people, and that justice will happen for all peoples.

We have prayed for justice for the Jewish people, who have suffered very deeply and who, in many parts of our own country, have played an important role in the struggle for justice and peace. We pray that they too, in their turn, will be able to be instruments of justice and peace. We pray that they will be able to be recognized as having a right to exist as an independent state, but that they will also hear the cries of the Palestinians who want an independent state.

4

During the pilgrimage Michael Nuttall, who was to develop a close partnership with Tutu, described his position as "number two to Tutu" and expressed the hope that they might be an icon for those they visited. Tutu took up the theme with the Franciscan monks who were the custodians of Christian holy places of Jerusalem.

If it can happen in South Africa that a black man and a white man can together be asked to be leaders of a church of God—in a country that is hagridden by hatred and racial animosity—then it can happen anywhere. If in South Africa you see the possibilities of reconciliation, then surely reconciliation should happen in other places—but especially here, in the place that gave birth to the one we call the Prince of Peace.

5

On Christmas Eve, Tutu preached at a carol service at Shepherds' Field, outside the village of Beit Sahour near Bethlehem, where residents were conducting a tax strike against the Israeli authorities as part of the first intifada, the Palestinian campaign of civil disobedience against Israeli occupation which had begun in 1987. The service drew thousands of Palestinians who, despite the presence of Israeli troops, turned the event into a demonstration in support of the Palestinian Liberation Organization.

Something stupendous, earth-shattering, happened in Bethlehem that first Christmas night: God's promised Messiah, God's own Son, was born in Bethlehem, and who were the first to be told the good news? It was not the high priest, not the king or his courtiers; it was shepherds watching their flock by night. Our people in South Africa love that story because it says shepherds are actually more important than the world thinks. Certainly, shepherds are important for God. Or even more wonderfully, the story says that God has a special caring for those whom the world thinks are not important. That God sides with those whom the world despises. That God sides with those whom the world brutalizes. That God is with those whom the world oppresses.

6

At a news conference after services at St. George's Cathedral in Jerusalem on Christmas Day, Tutu and Nuttall called for "true negotiations between the authentic representatives of both Israelis and Palestinians." Tutu also gave his views on the intifada.

I sympathize with the intifada insofar as it constitutes a strictly nonviolent and disciplined way of seeking justice. Palestinians and Israelis have an equal right to demand justice and self-determination. But as strongly as I identify with the striving of peoples for freedom, I deplore just as strongly the use of violence, whether it is the violence of those seeking to change the status quo or those seeking to uphold it. It is necessary, though, to go beyond vigorous denunciation of violence. We must go further by insisting on the removal of the conditions which are conducive to violence.

7

*On December 26, as the bishops left the cathedral to visit Yad
Vashem, the Holocaust museum, they saw that an outside wall had
been daubed overnight with a slogan reading, "Tutu is a black Nazi
pig." After a tour of the memorial, Tutu wrote his impressions in the
guestbook.*

It is a shattering experience, and the world must never forget
our inhumanity to one another. We pray that God would bless
all Jewish people and that they would be a light to the nations to
prevent such evil happening again. Forgive all people who oppress
others, dear God.

8

*Some Palestinian Anglicans were upset with Tutu for visiting Yad
Vashem. One protested that the treatment of Jews by Nazis was not
"the other side of the story" of the Palestinian-Israeli dispute. "We
were not responsible for the Holocaust," she said. At a meeting that
followed, an Israeli delegation led by Minister of Religious Affairs
Zevulun Hammer took particular exception to comparisons between
Israel's treatment of the Palestinians and the South African government's treatment of blacks. The visiting party included two Palestinians—Kafity and Anglican theologian Naim Ateek. Tutu spoke to
journalists afterward.*

I still feel that some of the things that I have seen on the occupied West Bank are things that I have seen at home. But I want to say that what is far more important is that we, coming out of our particular pain, could be used perhaps by God to enable people who have experienced pain in the past, who are experiencing pain now, to hear each other.

I have said to Israel's minister of religious affairs that we understand the anxieties, the apprehensions, the fears of the Jewish people. I have articulated that time and time again, saying that it is important for the Arabs, the Palestinians, to recognize Israel's right to a sovereign statehood; but equally, I would hope that the Israelis would hear the anguish and the cry of the Palestinians to equal recognition of their aspirations for sovereign statehood.

I will also say that when I find injustice and oppression anywhere in the world, whoever perpetrates it must know that I will condemn it. If I am accused, as I am often accused, of being anti-Semitic, tough luck. But I hope that we can be instruments of reconciliation and that this meeting has in fact enabled some Arabs, some Palestinians to speak to some Jews, Israelis.

9

Tutu's support for the Palestinian cause was met with a wave of criticism, particularly from Jewish groups in the United States. At the inauguration of David Dinkins as mayor of New York, shortly after Tutu's visit to Jerusalem, a protestor threw a water-filled balloon at the podium. Militants from the extremist Jewish Defense League in Southern California protested outside All Saints Church in Pasadena while Tutu was preaching there some months later.[4] In May 1990, during a Memorial Day weekend visit to Cincinnati, the Episcopal Diocese of Southern Ohio arranged a meeting between Tutu and a delegation headed by Alfred Gottschalk, president of the Hebrew Union College–Jewish Institute of Religion and a leading figure in Reform Judaism. After listening to members of the delegation raise their concerns about his views, Tutu gave an off-the-cuff reply, from which these excerpts are drawn.

Well, in some ways I am distressed myself that such a meeting should be thought to be necessary, and I think it *is* obviously necessary. Because, first, we have always recognized the outstanding record of members of the Jewish community—out of proportion to their numbers—in the struggle for justice in our country. And I want to express a warm tribute to yourselves for your part in that struggle—in some of the ways in which you have detailed here, your own personal involvement and the involvement of your institutions—and also your involvement in the civil rights movement in this country, because in many ways there's an important linkage. The relationships which have been warm between the Jewish and the African American communities are perhaps not as stable—I mean, they are in some jeopardy in my understanding of the situation, because of the question of the Israeli government.

I think it is going to be important for us in our discussions to make an important distinction between the Israeli government and

Jews. It's *very* important. It is important because the actions of the Israeli government are what is under scrutiny in relation to the Palestinian issue and also in relation to the Israeli government's relationship with the South African government. We cannot divorce consideration of relationships without making that point, and I think that is crucial.

Having said that, this next point is to say that what you might call our Jewish antecedents—if you don't want that, maybe then Hebrew antecedents—are a very serious part of my own makeup. My sermon yesterday was based almost exclusively, certainly initially, on a consideration of a key passage in the first book of what would also be the Hebrew scriptures: the account of the creation of human beings in the image of God. But it is not just that; it is my own being nurtured in the teaching of Israel's prophets, whom we have adopted as *our* prophets. It has been on the basis of what is central in my understanding of the teaching of what we call the Old Testament—the Law and Prophets and so on—that my own condemnations of injustice and oppression have been based.

In South Africa, I have spoken as a religious leader who has had that sort of formation. In other parts of Africa and in other parts of the world, my campaign, my passion, my zeal in seeking to speak up against evil and injustice has had that as a basis. And when I eventually visited the Holy Land last year, the things that I saw are things that I will not keep quiet over. That is when I said, If I am going to be accused of being anti-Semitic for saying them, then tough luck. And it's not out of an insensitivity. It is to say that I will not for myself accept that there is any government in the world that can claim to be infallible. If it is a human government, then it is a government that is likely to be making mistakes and can therefore, if it makes mistakes, be liable to criticism.

I speak as a black person who comes out of an experience of suffering because I am black. And therefore I know a little bit about what it means to suffer. My people know it. It doesn't matter that I hold the highest position in our church; in the land of my birth I am nothing because I am black. And therefore I speak out of that kind of experience of suffering. I saw things in the Holy Land and I was told things—things that have been reported widely, that you'll know of. I have not said so in public, but I have seen things there that shocked me. I mean, they've done awful things in South Africa, but I have not yet known of this practice that happens in the occupied territories: when a child in a home is suspected or let us say has been found to have thrown stones, the home of that child is bulldozed or that home is sealed. Now I would want to ask you whether, just as caring people, you approve of the things that the Israeli government does.

Now I have spoken about one of the wonderful things in Israel. You know after that awful thing that happened in Shatila—yes, one thing that we mentioned with a sense of pride was that half a million Jews demonstrated against Israel's involvement. Now that is something that would not have happened certainly in South Africa, for instance, and it was something that we mentioned as a point when we're saying: this is how we understand Jews would be. We assume, because of your peculiar experience and the peculiarity of who you are, that there is a sense in which—and you may say that that is unfair—a sense in which there are things we would not expect would happen. That is part of what I have been saying, and I would hope that you would join me in condemning what is wrong in the actions of the government of Israel and not assume that when a person says that, that you have opposition to Jews. I will not deny that I have said you need only to change the names and you would think that you were having a description of what was happening in South Africa. I'm speaking as a black person and I am not accusing Jews. I am accusing the Israeli government. And I would want to know whether you in fact approve of the things that happen there in the name of the people of Israel.

But let me also just say, as a black South African, that Israel is going to have to determine whether it is on our side or not, in the struggle in South Africa. Israel has assisted in our repression through what it has done in its cooperation with the South African government over security issues. I'm not going to keep quiet about that. And I'm not attacking Jews. I'm attacking a government that happens to be Jewish. I will not stop saying so. And black people at home need to be told how it is possible for a government of people who suffered under Nazism to cooperate with a government, most of whose members were Nazi sympathizers, against black people who fought against Hitler. We would want to know what you expect our attitude to that government to be.

The position I'm taking on the Middle East issue and the Palestinian question is not in fact a personal position, or let me say my personal position coincides with the position of the Anglican Communion. The resolution that was taken at the Lambeth Conference in 1988 is a resolution that says two important things: one, we deplore as you do the fact that Arab countries over a long period of time refused to recognize that Israel existed and were working to destroy Israel. And so we recognize the right of Israel to exist as a sovereign, independent state whose security is guaranteed, whose territorial integrity is guaranteed and recognized internationally. The other part of the resolution is calling for hearing the cry of the Palestinians for an independent, sovereign state. Now this is not to pretend that at one time they did not have opportunities of doing much of what they're now crying for. That is water under the bridge. We are saying we are at this point. And I am quite serious about the offer of wanting, if Eli Wiesel wanted to, for us as Nobel Peace laureates to make ourselves available in whatever way would advance the course of reconciliation.

10

After the meeting, Tutu summarized his feelings to journalists.

The important thing is that where there is injustice, we should be able to say together, Yes, that is an unjust occurrence, and not quickly say, Because So-and-So criticizes that aspect, therefore they are anti-Semitic. I mean, I criticize Mrs. Margaret Thatcher fairly sharply, but I've not usually been called anti-British for doing so.[5] At home we walk arm in arm with rabbis when we go on demonstrations against apartheid, and I would hope that we would agree that the things that hold us together are far, far greater than the things that conspire to separate us.

11

The easing of tensions in the Middle East after the Oslo Accords were signed in 1993 was followed by an improvement in Tutu's relations with his Israeli and Jewish critics for some years. Soon after presiding over the South African Truth and Reconciliation Commission, he was given a friendly reception by both Israelis and Palestinians when in 1999 he visited Tel Aviv—at the invitation of fellow Nobel laureate Shimon Peres—and the West Bank—invited by the local Anglican bishop. In Jerusalem, Israeli peace activists wanted to hear in particular about reconciliation and forgiveness in South Africa. However, Tutu's relations with Israel's supporters, particularly in the United States, deteriorated after the collapse of the Middle East peace process, to the degree that phrases he used in admonitions to both apartheid leaders and the democratically elected South African administrations began to be repeated in his speeches on the Middle East. In 2002, he was invited by American supporters of Jerusalem's Sabeel Ecumenical Liberation Theology Center, a Palestinian Christian group founded by Naim Ateek, one of the hosts of his 1989 Christmas pilgrimage, to address a meeting in Old South Church, Boston. He began his presentation by taking issue with the title he had been given for his address: "Occupation Is Oppression."

I would like for us to have changed that and said, "Give Peace a Chance, For Peace Is Possible." You see, we are bearers of hope for God's children in the Holy Land, for God's people the Israeli Jews and God's people the Palestinian Arabs. We want to say to them, Our hearts go out to all who have suffered as a result of the violence of suicide bombers and the violence of military incursions and reprisals, and we express our deepest sympathies to all who have been injured and bereaved in the horrendous events of recent times. We want to say to all involved in the events of these past days, Peace is possible. Israeli Jew, Palestinian Arab can live amicably side by side in a secure peace—and, as Canon Naim Ateek kept underscoring, a secure peace built on justice and equity. These two peoples are God's chosen and beloved, looking in their faiths back to a common ancestor, Abraham, and confessing belief in the one creator God of Salaam and Shalom.

I give thanks for all that I have received as a Christian from the teachings of God's people the Jews. When we were opposing the vicious system of apartheid, which claimed that what invested people with worth was a biological irrelevance—skin color—we turned to the Jewish Torah, which asserted that what gave people their infinite worth was the fact that they were created in the image of God. Thus, on this score, apartheid was unbiblical, evil without remainder, and therefore unchristian.

And when our people groaned by virtue of the burden of racist oppression, we invoked the God who addressed Moses in the burning bush. We told our people that our God had heard their cry, had seen their anguish, and knew their suffering, and would come down—this great God of the Exodus, the liberator God—as in the past to deliver us as God had delivered Israel from bondage. We told them that God was biased in favor of those without clout— the poor, the weak, the hungry, the voiceless—as God had shown when God intervened through the prophet Nathan against King David on behalf of Uriah, Bathsheba's husband. Or as God intervened through Elijah on behalf of Naboth, against King Ahab and Jezebel when they confiscated Naboth's vineyard and caused Naboth to be killed.

We said that this God would never abandon us, for when we were thrown into the fiery furnace of tribulation and suffering caused by apartheid, this God would be there with us as Emmanuel, "God with us," just as this God had been there with Daniel and his companions. We said that this God rejected worship which did not change the lives and conduct of the worshippers, to make them care especially for the widow, the orphan, and the alien, those who in most societies are among the most vulnerable and least influential; that this God preferred obedience to sacrifice, doing mercy rather than sacrifice, making justice flow like a river, walking humbly with God. And this God called on God's people always to remember that they had been aliens and slaves in Egypt, and this memory would galvanize them and inspire them to be in their turn compassionate and generous with the alien in their midst.

We would invoke the Jewish scriptures that have asserted that this was God's world and, despite all appearances to the contrary, God was in charge; that this was, therefore, a moral universe. There was no way in which might could ever be right; that injus-

tice, lies, oppression could never have the last word in the universe
of this God.

In our struggle against apartheid, some of the most outstanding
stalwarts were Jews: the Helen Suzmans, the Joe Slovos, the Albie
Sachses.[6] As in this country in the civil rights movement, Jews
almost instinctively, as a matter of course—given their religious
traditions, their history—had to be on the side of the disenfran-
chised, the discriminated against, the voiceless ones fighting injustice, oppression, and evil. I have continued to feel strongly with the
Jews and with many other Nobel Peace laureates. I am a member
of the board of the Peres Center for Peace in Tel Aviv. I am a patron
of the Cape Town Holocaust Centre. I believe that Israel has a right
to secure borders, internationally recognized, in a land assured of
territorial integrity and with acknowledged sovereignty as an independent country; that the Arab nations made a bad mistake in
refusing to recognize the existence of sovereign Israel and in pledg-
ing to work for her destruction. It was a shortsighted policy that led
to Israel's nervousness and her high state of alertness and military
preparedness to guarantee her continued existence. This was understandable. What was not so understandable, not justifiable, was
what Israel did to another people to guarantee her existence.

I have been very deeply distressed in all my visits to the Holy
Land by how so much of what was taking place there reminded me
so much of what used to happen to us blacks in apartheid South
Africa. I have seen the humiliation of the Palestinians at the roadblocks and recalled what used to happen to us in our motherland,
when arrogant, young white police officers would hector and bully

us, and demean us when we ran the gauntlet of their unpredict-
able whims—whether they would let us through or not; when they
seemed to derive so much fun out of our sullen humiliation. I have
seen such scenes, or heard of them, being played out in the Holy
Land. The rough and discourteous demands for IDs from the Palestinians were so uncannily reminiscent of the infamous pass-law
raids of the vicious apartheid regime.[7]

We saw on those visits, or read about, things that did not
happen even in apartheid South Africa: the demolition of homes
because of a suspicion that one or other family member was a ter-
rorist, and so *all* paid a price in these acts of collective punishment,
seemingly being repeated more recently in the attacks on Arab
refugee camps. We don't know the exact truth because the Israelis
won't let the media in. What are they hiding? But perhaps, more
seriously, why is there no outcry in this country at the censor-
ship of their media? For you see, what now is going to happen is
that you will frequently be shown the harrowing images of what
suicide bombers have done, which is something we all condemn
unequivocally, but you don't see what those tanks are doing to the
homes of ordinary people.

On one of my visits to the Holy Land, I drove one Sunday to
a church service with the Anglican bishop of Jerusalem. We went
past Ramallah. I could hear the tears in his voice as he pointed to
the Jewish settlements. I thought of the desire of the Israelis for
security, and the anguish of the Palestinians at the land they have
lost, the occupation that has said they are nothing, they count for
nothing. That pain and the many humiliations that have been suf-

fered are fertile soil for the desperation of suicide bombers. I was walking with Canon Ateek, whose father was a jeweler, and as we walked in Jerusalem he pointed out and said, "Our home was over there. We were driven out of our home. It is now occupied by Israeli Jews." And then I recalled how many times people of color would point in South Africa in much the same way to their former homes from which they had been expelled and which were now inhabited by whites. My heart aches.

I say, Why are our memories so short? Have our Jewish sisters and brothers forgotten the humiliation of wearing yellow armbands with the star of David? Have my Jewish sisters and brothers forgotten the collective punishment? The home demolitions? Have they forgotten their own history so soon? And have they turned their back on their profound, noble religious traditions? Have they forgotten that their God, our God, is a God who sides with the poor, the despised, the downtrodden? That this is a moral universe? That they will never—they will *never*—get true security and safety from the barrel of a gun? That true peace can ultimately be built only on justice and equity?

We condemn the violence of suicide bombers, and if Arab children are taught to hate Jews, we condemn the corruption of young minds too. But we condemn equally unequivocally the violence of military incursions and reprisals that won't let ambulances and medical personnel reach the injured; that wreak unparalleled revenge, totally imbalanced, even with the Torah's law of an eye for an eye—which was designed actually to restrict revenge to the perpetrator and perhaps those supporting him. It is the humiliation and desperation of an occupied and hapless people which are the root causes of the suicide bombings. The military action of recent days—I want to predict with almost absolute certainty—will not provide the security and the peace the Israelis want. All it is doing is intensifying the hatred and the resentment and guaranteeing that one day a suicide bomber will arise to wreak revenge.

Israel has three options: to revert to the stalemate of the recent status quo, bristling with tension, hatred, and violence; or to perpetuate genocide and exterminate all Palestinians; or third, which is what I hope they will choose, to strive for peace based on justice based on withdrawal from all the occupied territories. And the Palestinians must be committed too, and say so loud and clear at every opportunity: that they too are committed to such a peace. We in South Africa had a situation where everyone thought we would be overwhelmed by a bloodbath. It did not happen. We had a relatively peaceful transition. And instead of revenge and retribution we had the remarkable process of forgiveness and reconciliation of the Truth and Reconciliation Commission. If our madness, if our intractable problem, could have ended as it did, then we believe it must be possible everywhere else in the world. For South Africa is, yes, an unlikely candidate, but South Africa is this beacon of hope, beacon of hope for the rest of the world. If it could happen in South Africa, it can happen anywhere else. If peace could come in South Africa, then surely it can come in the Holy Land.

Sometimes people ask, "Does this mean you are pro-Palestinian?" And my brother Naim Ateek has said what we used to say too: I am not pro–this or that people; I am pro-justice. I am pro-freedom. I am anti-injustice, anti-oppression any- and everywhere that it occurs. But you know as well as I do that somehow the Israeli government is placed on a pedestal, where to criticize them is immediately to be dubbed anti-Semitic—as if the Palestinians were not Semitic. I have not been even anti-white, despite all the suffering that that crazy group inflicted on our people. No! How could I be—if I wasn't even anti–those who did that to us—anti-Jew? Because that is actually the term that ought to be used: Are you anti-Jewish? Not anti-Semitic. And then you would have to say the same thing to the biblical prophets, because they were some of the most scathing critics of the Jewish leadership of their day. We don't criticize Jewish *people*. We criticize, we will criticize, when they need to be criticized, the *government* of Israel.

People are scared in this country to say wrong is wrong. Because the Jewish lobby is powerful, very powerful. So what? So what! This is God's world! For goodness' sake, this is God's world! The apartheid government was very powerful, but we said to them, Watch it! If you flout the laws of this universe, you're going to bite the dust! Hitler was powerful. Mussolini was powerful. Stalin was powerful. Idi Amin was powerful. Pinochet was powerful. The apartheid government was powerful. Milošević was powerful.

But this is God's world. A lie, injustice, oppression—those will never prevail in the world of this God. That is what we told our people. And we used to say, Those ones, they have already lost. We may not be around. An unjust Israeli government, however powerful, will fall in the world of this kind of God. We don't want that to happen, but those who are powerful have to remember the litmus test that God gives to the powerful: What is your treatment of the poor, the hungry? What is your treatment of the vulnerable, the voiceless? And on the basis of that, God passes God's judgment.

We should put out a clarion call. Let's make a clarion call to the government of the people of Israel, a clarion call to the Palestinian people, and say, Peace is possible! Peace based on justice is possible! And we are meeting today, and we will continue going on, calling for this, for your own sake, Israeli Jews, for your own sake, Palestinian Arabs. Peace is possible, and we will do all we can to assist you in achieving this peace which is within your grasp, because it is God's dream that you will be able to live amicably together as sisters and brothers, side by side, because you belong in God's family. Peace! Peace! Peace!

The Boston Globe *reported later that Jewish leaders reacted strongly to Tutu's remarks. "It's tragic that a person of his moral credentials would sacrifice them with such an ugly slur," the newspaper quoted Rob Leikind, director of the New England chapter of the Anti-Defamation League, as saying. "Israel is in a simple fight for survival. It's a sad day for all of us when people engage in that kind of hyperbole."*

PART THREE

Voice of South Africa's Voiceless

CHAPTER 10

Why Black?

A Defense of Black Theology

A decade before Desmond Tutu's ministry took on international dimensions, and twenty years before he became known as an apostle of tolerance and forgiveness, it was for his attacks on apartheid that he first won renown. An early example of the passion and bluntness—even abrasiveness, Tutu acknowledged—for which he was later to become known is to be found in a paper on black theology that he wrote for a conference on Southern Africa held in Britain in 1973. Tutu grew up in a family and community committed to the ideal of a society in which race would not determine how society was organized. This commitment was reinforced by a stay in London in the mid-1960s, during which he studied theology at King's College, London. However, when he returned home to teach at a South African theological college in 1967, he encountered a new phenomenon among his students: the fast-spreading black consciousness movement, through which young intellectuals such as the medical student Steve Biko were trying to revolutionize black society. While the movement did not repudiate the objective of a nonracial society, it held that, as a consequence of generations of educational and other discrimination, black South Africans operated at a disadvantage in interacting with whites, and that they would continue to do so unless they withdrew from multiracial organizations and built up their self-confidence and their power base until they could engage with whites as equals. In his 1973 paper, Tutu rejected as irrelevant, for himself and the people to whom he ministered, the "God is dead" movement that had swept Western theological institutions in the late 1960s, proudly asserting his black identity and integrating into his thinking the principles of black consciousness. At the same time, within his argument can be discerned his underlying commitment to a vision of a shared humanity, alive to the possibility that the oppressed are as liable to sin as the oppressor and believing that the liberation of the black person is inextricably bound up with that of the white. (Also apparent in these early writings is the sexist language to which Tutu refers in the foreword, which for the most part has been left unaltered.)

A strange phenomenon has appeared on the intellectual landscape and has caused some consternation or aroused some interest among those who have cared to note its appearance. Many in the West, however, have just ignored it. The strange phenomenon I refer to is black theology. Some of those who have ignored it have asked, apparently reasonably, "How can you have a black theology? Surely this is as absurd as to speak of white or European physics or chemistry or mathematics?"

These rhetorical questions are not as devastating as intended by those who pose them. It is true that it appears odd to apply ethnic or racial epithets to such aspects of human endeavor as science. But it is not nearly so unusual to discern national or racial characteristics in other kinds of human activity and to describe these appropriately. It is not thought odd, for instance, to speak of British or German or European art, music, or philosophy. It is not unusual to see references to German or American theology. Why should it be thought odd a priori to speak of black theology? One more than half suspects that those who react negatively or with a poorly disguised hauteur to the term "black theology" have already made up their minds that there could not be any such preposterous entity. As somebody aptly put it, when they ask, "What is black theology?" they are really asking, "Is black theology, theology at all?" I will try to answer this question later.

Let us deal at the moment with "Why black?" Most reactions to blackness are negative ones. This is borne out to a great extent by language. When one is in a rotten mood, then one is in a black mood; the bad exception is the black sheep. In most Christian religious art, the good angels are white, the devil and his angels are black. Black is generally associated with death; white, with purity and life. This is in fact true, even in some of the linguistic usage of Africa. The Motswana wishing one bon voyage will, in his own language, say, "Have a white road." The trouble with all those cultural reactions and customs is how easily they help to condition humans. It starts off as an innocent enough human characteristic, but soon it develops, as it has most certainly done in this instance, to a general denigration of things black and of black persons. When this happens for long enough, it is not long before you, a black person, wonder whether you are not as they depict you. You begin, deep down, to have doubts about your own humanity. It sounds melodramatic. I wish it were. Unfortunately, it is only too true.

The point is that we blacks have been defined too often in the white man's terms: we are *non*-white, *non*-European—negatives. Language has a potent relationship to reality. From being thought of or spoken about as "non-this" or "non-that" we end up being treated as nonentities. Maybe that is too strong. Well, we end up being treated as human but not quite as human as the white man, or, what amounts to the same thing, we are treated as inferior persons, not quite on the same level as those who deign to notice our existence. What is more serious is that we begin to think of ourselves in the way we have come to be commonly described.

We have now adopted the term "black" quite deliberately so that we can describe ourselves positively. It is an assertion of our personhood, our identity in its own right, not merely over and against anybody else. We are declaring to ourselves or to anybody who cares to listen that we are fundamentally subjects not objects, persons not things. Each of us is an "I," not an "it." We have to say this over and over again to "unbrainwash" ourselves, until we believe it and can act as if we really did believe in our own dignity and humanity.

The trouble is that the white man has, up to now, perhaps unconsciously yet certainly, sought to determine our existence. He has, as it were, drawn up the agenda for our lives. We have hitherto been playing a game whose rules have been determined by the white man, and he has often even been the referee as well. So we use "black" as an epithet here because we are black: because we are each somebody. We matter, we're alive and kicking, and black *is* beautiful.

Is Black Theology, Theology?

The white man has quite arrogantly believed that his standards were of universal validity. This has not normally been asserted in so many words. No, it has been taken as part of the nature of things, too obvious to be declared. It has just been taken as read. This has included theological reflection and expression. We might get a spate of denials against this charge, but it remains true that political and economic power have given the white man considerable leverage to exercise cultural and intellectual neocolonialism even where there has been political decolonization.

By and large, what the West decides as counting for, say, academic excellence is academic excellence for the rest of the world. This has occurred in theology as well. Black theology is a repudiation of this Western arrogance. Black theology makes the proper assertion to which Anglo-Saxon theology at least pays lip service: that there can never be a final theology, for theology changes as various ingredients in the mixture change—the life experience of the particular community, its self-understanding, its manner and categories of expression. Anglo-Saxon theology tends to lay claim to a universality it can never properly possess. This is because theology is an attempt to make sense of the life experience of a particular Christian community, a community conditioned by time and space, and all of this in relation to what God has done or is doing and will do—the fundamental reference point being the man Jesus.

Each proper theology must take the scandal of its own particularity seriously. Therein lies its strengths and its limitations. It speaks out of and to a specific context. To that extent it is contextual and existential. The trouble is that most of the theology we blacks have imbibed in theological institutions has been trying to speak to the conditions and in terms of the white man. I am prepared to concede that all the effort spent on discussing the erudite concerns of linguistic philosophical theology, or the "death of God" theology, is spent usefully in dealing with the vital questions that plague the ordinary white man. That is the legitimate concern of white theology—"white" because such it is and has been, however vehemently its practitioners may care to deny it. Actually, if they were right that theirs is not a white theology, then they have no business to be Christian theologians, since they would not be doing their job, which is to reflect on the experience of a particular community in the light of Christian revelation.

The point I am at such pains to labor is that Christians do not apprehend the mysteries of their faith in exactly the same way, and they express their different understanding in diverse ways. Consequently, there will be different theologies limited by the limitations and distortions of their particularities. A good theology must recognize its built-in obsolescence. God speaks to us as we are, and our theology is filtered through who we are.

Black theology is an engaged theology, not an academic, detached theology. It is a gut-level theology, relating to the real concerns, the life-and-death issues of the black man. If the white man is so made that he finds it genuinely difficult to understand the meaning of apparently straightforward sentences such as "God loves you," then perhaps the white theologian is justified in being concerned with Wittgenstein—with the verification principle et al. The black theologian can dabble in these philosophical, semantic games only cerebrally, enjoying the exhilaration of being able to perform adroitly in this kind of intellectual gymnastics. But this is not what touches the heart of the black experience.

Black theology seeks to make sense of the life experience of the black man, which is largely black suffering at the hands of rampant white racism, and to understand this in the light of what God has said about himself, about man, and about the world in his definitive Word. Black theology has to do with whether it is possible to be black and continue to be Christian; it is to ask on whose side is God; it is to be concerned about the humanization of persons, because those who ravage our humanity dehumanize themselves in the process; it is concerned with the liberation of all, black and white, since the liberation of the black man is the other side of the coin of the liberation of the white man. It is a clarion call for man to align himself with the God who is the God of Exodus, God the liberator, who leads his people, all his people, out of all kinds of bondage—political, economic, cultural; out of the bondage of sin and disease—into the glorious liberty of the sons of God.

When we practice black theology, we no longer use "black" as merely an ethnic epithet. It refers to all who are oppressed in any way and who are ready to appropriate for themselves the insights of black theology insofar as these are relevant to their own particular life situation. Black theology is thus the theology of the oppressed, and to this extent it is a theology of liberation. It seeks to lay bare for all to see that the divine activity is in fact ultimately of a piece: God sets his people free to enter the Promised Land in *this* life and not merely in some vague celestial future. It claims that God is forever active in upsetting the status quo. Humanity's future is not determined. It is open to the divine surprise, which subverts dehumanizing structures which make God's children less than what he intends them to be.

Does black theology lay claim to a universality which it has been so quick to condemn in others? No, it does not seek to impose its forms, its insights, its deliverances, on anybody. On the contrary, it joyously celebrates its particularity, for only thus can it carry out its appointed task. It has no illusions about its own limitations, which must by definition be inherent in its very nature. It nowhere wishes to canonize its own necessary parochialism; it cannot disclaim its particularity and still retain its integrity.

This is what we understand by black theology, a theology which is concerned to reconcile the overwhelming experience of black people with what black Christians have come to accept are the nature and activity of God as supremely revealed in Our Lord and Savior. Jesus Christ in a real sense was not any and every man. To have been really and truly man he had to be a particular man, born of a particular woman at a particular time and in a particular place. Only thus could he then be universalized, but with considerable caution because some things he did and said were relative and much harm has happened to the Christian enterprise in attempting to make absolute the relative. The divine *kenosis* (self-emptying) had to occur for the incarnation to be God really truly becoming man. And always God left himself open to being misunderstood.

For us it is a matter of life and death in the Johannine sense that we engage seriously in black theology. Our existence as Christians is at stake. We must see whether God is, as the scriptures depict him to be, the God of the Magnificat, who fills the hungry with good things, who sends the rich away empty; whether indeed he is the God who sent his Son and continues to send his sons "to bring good news to the humble, to bind up the broken-hearted, to proclaim liberty to captives and release to those in prison, . . . to comfort all who mourn, to give them garlands instead of ashes, oil of gladness instead of mourners' tears, a garment of splendor for the heavy heart" (Luke 1:46–55; Isaiah 61:1–3, NEB).

For us it is an existential question. And we will not be baulked by those who may sidetrack us by wanting to scrutinize the academic bona fides of the enterprise. Frankly, the time has passed when we will wait for the white man to give us permission to do our thing. Whether or not he accepts the intellectual respectability of our activity is largely irrelevant. We will proceed, regardless. This does not mean we will not attempt to be self-critical. No, the matter in hand is too serious to be treated shoddily or in any offhand way. We are fully aware that the answers black theology can give will be only false palliatives if they suffer from such weaknesses as internal self-contradiction. Black theology must follow the evidence wherever it leads and face up to issues and problems squarely without cooking the solutions. But we refuse to be told what issues we should pursue, or the forms in which we may express the results of our theologizing and reflection. We too can be trusted with having some grasp of the Christian verities and with knowing that what black theology delivers should, in the final analysis, be consistent with the deliverance of scripture, with what we discern of God in the face of Jesus Christ.

But black theology must speak its own language to those whom it is primarily addressing: blacks. That language may shock others for being intemperate, unscholarly, bizarre—for example, "Jesus is black." Black has a rich and emotive cluster of meanings. We will not be dismissed by arrogant misreadings of the surface meaning of our theological statements. We will not be deterred in doing what we must do. This is not a plea for acceptance nor an attempt at demonstrating the academic respectability of black theology. No, it is just a straightforward, perhaps shrill statement about an existent. Black theology *is*. No permission is being requested for it to come into being. Perhaps one day it may receive something like the attention being showered on Pentecostalism, which has become respectable now that it is affecting Westerners in great numbers, and which has been a religious phenomenon in, for instance, Africa for decades.

The Implications of Black Theology

Black theology incidentally challenges most other theology to be truly more biblical. It asserts that all theology should be engaged, in that it must deal with the burning life issues of the particular Christian community whose experience forms an integral and authentic part of the data of that theology. When we examine the Bible, we find that most of the theology it contains, especially in the New Testament, is as it were forged in the heat of battle, almost on the battlefield itself. It is occasional in the technical sense of being occasioned by a particular set of circumstances, and it seeks to be relevant to those circumstances. It tries to answer pressing questions arising from them, to assuage the pain and anguish of living in them; it tries to incorporate knowledge from man's attempts to understand other aspects of himself and the universe he inhabits, and to assimilate this into as coherent a whole as possible, so that members of this community can live with a reasonable measure of integrity. Most of the New Testament was written to deal with situations of deep perplexity and even anguish. Are you really a Christian if you are not circumcised, or are you outside the pale? Can a Jewish Christian be expected to fraternize with a Gentile Christian? Has the resurrection happened or not? If the Old Testament gave all these prophecies about Jesus Christ, how did it happen that the Jews failed to recognize him? In becoming a Christian, did not a Jew forfeit something that was far superior to the new faith he was now accepting? If God were truly the ruler of all and Christ had overcome all enemies, why was the archenemy of the Christian so powerful still and why were Christians suffering so much—was God inactive, indifferent, powerless?

Black theology is attempting to do for a significant sector of Christianity precisely what the biblical authors were doing for the communities to which they addressed themselves. Since the occasions were various, the theologies which were produced and recorded in the Bible are themselves varied. Because of their particularity they must of necessity display a rich diversity. Who can seriously argue that the New Testament would be greatly improved if the four Gospels had been thoroughly harmonized into one account? Or that the books of Job and Ruth do not add a necessary counterbalance to Ezra-Nehemiah? That we do not on the whole possess in the Bible a far more wonderful thing with prophecy cheek by jowl with apocalypse, each genre with its own particular brand of theology? We risk losing a splendid richness if we decry the existence of many varied theologies in pursuing our desire for a premature universality and unity. Biblical unity comes not out of a uniformity of style or understanding, but from being centered on God's action in human history, on the record of this activity and of man's understanding of, distortion of, and response to this activity.

Another level at which black theology challenges other theologies to be biblical is in its concern for the whole person. The Bible, as well as Christianity at its best, is materialistic in the proper sense. The prophets had an apparently stubborn inability to separate the marketplace or the judicial village gate from the temple and the sanctuary. Many of today's Christians, especially those who enjoy positions of affluence or political power, seem to be obtuse about the relevance of their faith to political, economic, and social conditions. Christianity is ultimately going to lose any credibility it may still possess if it is seen to be in alliance with oppressive political and economic forces upholding an unjust status quo. There may be some among the oppressed who use Christianity as a form of escapism from harsh reality, but there is a growing number for whom disillusionment is corroding their faith. Preaching pie in the sky when you die is an insult to God.

Black theology throws out a challenge to so-called African theology. For far too long African theology has seemed concerned to show that Africa has an authentic religious heritage, to serve as a bridge between African consciousness and Christianity. But that cannot be the sum total of African theology. It must now begin to address itself far more seriously to the issues which concern the contemporary African. It must grapple with the enormous problems that have come in the train of political independence. It must have something to say about the theology of power, of underdevelopment, of political coups, of elitism. It must be concerned about the intransigence of human nature. Black theology is not so naïve as to think that white oppression is the only bondage from which blacks need to be liberated. Sin and evil are as dehumanizing as white racism, and when the white oppressor in Africa is removed, he is far too often succeeded by his black counterpart. African theology has not yet delivered anything significant on this and other contemporary issues. To begin to do this it will have to take up the challenge of black theology.

In sum, then, black theology is concerned for the whole of the black man, to help him to come to terms with his own existence, to speak to his particular condition and to help him to assert his own personhood, and to enter into his inalienable heritage as a child of God and an inheritor of the kingdom of heaven. It seeks to help him to become ever more what God intends him to be, a human person liberated from all kinds of bondage which have dehumanized him. This after all is why Christ came: "I am come that they might have life and that they might have it in all its abundance" (John 10:10).

CHAPTER 11

I Stand Here Before You

Why Christians Must Be Involved in Politics

*Desmond Tutu was first propelled into the public arena when he was
chosen, in quick succession, as the first black dean of Johannesburg
(in 1975), as Anglican bishop of the neighboring state of Lesotho
(1976), and then as general secretary of the South African Council
of Churches (1978). In an era in which the principal forces fighting apartheid had been driven underground or into exile, and their
leaders jailed, the pulpits of the churches provided public platforms
from which black South Africans could speak freely, and the meetings
of their ruling bodies one of the few forums in which black and white
could debate as relative equals. From the beginning of his public life,
Tutu stood out immediately for his uncompromising advocacy of the
aspirations of black South Africans, unencumbered by euphemism,
defiant in the face of the apparatus of a police state, but at the same
time sensitive to the anxieties of his white fellow church leaders. At
a time when the imprisoned Nelson Mandela and Mandela's friend*

*and one-time law partner Oliver Tambo—the exiled leader of the
African National Congress (ANC)—were demonized by the apartheid government as terrorists, Tutu was among a tiny minority of
voices willing to advocate for their ideals, publicly, boldly, and passionately, to both black and white audiences.*

1

*This speech was prepared for a white audience late in 1978, two years
after the landmark national youth rebellion that was set off by the
schoolchildren of Soweto.*

I stand here before you as one who professes to be a Christian.
That is the starting point for everything that I am; it is the inspi-
ration for all that I say and do. As a Christian therefore I place, as
that which has my absolute loyalty and as having a first position in
my life, the worship and services of God. I want to underline that
my priority is to glorify and to praise God. I must have an authentic relationship first with God through prayer, through Bible reading, through meditation and using the sacraments of the church. I
therefore place the spiritual as having an overriding importance in
my life. This is the so-called vertical dimension of human life, this
relationship with God.

But that is not the end—it could not be the end. The authenticity of this vertical relationship, this spiritual relationship with

God, is expressed for me and tested out by my relationship with my neighbor. This is the so-called horizontal dimension. The vertical and the horizontal must be held together. Our Lord and Master Jesus Christ said, "Thou shalt love the Lord thy God with all thy heart, and with all thy soul, and with all thy mind. This is the first and great commandment. And the second is like unto it— thou shalt love thy neighbor as thyself" (Matthew 22:36–40, KJV). For Jesus, love of God was inconceivable and could not exist without its corollary love of neighbor. One of the evangelists sums up the teaching of the Bible in this matter by asking, "How can you say you love God whom you have not seen if you hate the brother whom you have seen?" (1 John 4:20).

What I am saying is that I am not a politician. It is not my politics that causes me to be involved in the sociopolitical arena. No, it is my Christian belief. It is because I too think I have had an encounter with Jesus Christ in prayer, in Bible reading, and it is precisely this encounter which constrains me to say and to do the things that I say and do. It is in obedience to the imperative of the gospel of Jesus Christ, to the commandment of God, and to the teaching of the Bible that I am involved in sociopolitical and economic matters. And for this I do not apologize at all. I reject all false dichotomies as between the sacred and the secular about things that are called religious and others that are merely secular. For me religion is concerned about all of life and not only about certain aspects of it. The God whom I worship is the Lord of all life. There is no aspect of human existence where his writ does not run.

In a parable about the Last Judgment, Jesus Christ teaches that we will be judged about whether we are fit for heaven or hell by whether we did or did not do certain things. It is interesting that all these things could not strictly be called religious: feeding the hungry, visiting the sick, clothing the naked, visiting prisoners in prison.

I do not lay claim to an infallibility no human being can rightly possess, and therefore I admit that I can be wrong. But I must say quite categorically that as soon as I am clear that in any one given situation the demands of the gospel of Jesus Christ are such and such, then I can do no other; and consequently it is in obedience to what I understand to be the will of God that I will do and say whatever I think needs to be said or done. I do not seek a confrontation with the authorities, but once I have decided, I will not constantly look over my shoulder to see whether I have the approbation or otherwise of the authorities, or of other fellow Christians who may think differently and who may be powerful. I would much rather obey God than men.

We long that our appeal, our *cri de coeur*, will be heard by our government and by our white fellow South Africans. I speak out of a deep love for my beloved country and a concern for my white fellow countrymen. I say, Please, let us sit together, black and white, all the authentic and acknowledged leaders of the different sections of our community—I say "acknowledged" and not leaders who are imposed on us—let us parley with one another before the cause of reasonably peaceful change is irretrievably lost. The former South African prime minister, Mr. B. J. Vorster, rightly advised Mr. Ian

Smith[1] to start talking with black leaders, to release those he had
detained, and to try to hammer out a negotiated settlement. Mr.
Vorster advised those in Namibia to get together around a conference table and talk and to seek together a just settlement in that
territory. Why does he think that this way of going about things
should be only for export? Why should we not do our thing here
at home as well while there may just still be the outside chance
that we can work out, all of us black and white together, the kind
of future we want for our land: to deliver a blueprint for a more
open, more just, more equitable society, where persons count because they are human beings made in the image of God and not
because of biological and historical accidents such as the amount of
melanin in their skin.

You know, all our most outstanding black leaders from time im-
memorial have declared that they don't want to drive you whites
into the sea, because we belong together, black and white, to
mother South Africa, and they have all stretched out a hand of
fellowship toward whites. So far they have met with nothing but
rebuff after rebuff. The miracle of South Africa is that blacks still
talk to whites after what has happened to us over three centuries,
ghastly treatment that has become worse since the formal introduc-
tion of apartheid in 1948. Talk with us and stop talking about us.

I must issue a warning as soberly and as responsibly as I can. If
the present order of things continues in this land, then as sure as
day follows night we will have a bloodbath in this beautiful country. Please, there can be no real and lasting security for whites in
South Africa as long as the vast majority of South Africa's inhabi-

tants are not free. Whites can have no real and lasting security based on military and police power as long as the vast majority of South African citizens see the good resources of the land of their birth distributed so unfairly. There can be no real freedom for whites in this land until blacks are free, for whites have to spend enormous resources trying to safeguard their separate freedom, and freedom, my friends, is indivisible.

As a Christian I believe that God cares about justice, about righteousness, about right and wrong, about exploitation, about oppression. And I know that the South African way of life, the present ordering of society, is unjust and immoral. It is oppressive and evil. If whites don't think so, could they please change places with blacks for a few days? Let them leave their posh homes and come to stay in Soweto and use the inadequate means of transport; let them run the gauntlet of police roadblocks; let them be subject to the multifarious laws which apply to blacks for just a few days, and see whether they don't agree that this system is evil, is unjust and immoral and for that reason is bound to fail. Because God finds it hateful in his sight. Don't delude yourselves. It is an unchristian system, abhorrent to Christian consciences in the rest of the world, and it will collapse like all other immoral systems before it—systems which appeared to carry all before them.

You, my white brothers and sisters, must know that you are being asked to support a system that is utterly indefensible. Abandon it before it is too late. You, my white brothers and sisters, must know that once a people decide that they will become free, then nothing, absolutely nothing, in the world will stop them reaching the goal of self-determination—not all the military and police power in the world. In recent times Vietnam has shown this. The former Portuguese colonies have shown this. But much, much closer at hand, the Afrikaners are a living proof of this in their own history. Why do they think that we blacks will be the exception to a universal law?

Change—not cosmetic alterations, but real and radical change—is coming about; of that there is no doubt. What are still open to question are how and when this change will happen, and you, my white brothers and sisters, alone must answer those questions.

I appeal to you: please hear us. All we want is for you to recognize that we are human beings like you—we laugh and cry; we love and marry just like you; we want justice as you do; we want peace just like you; we want reconciliation. We want to avert bloody violence just like you. But those of us among black leaders who speak about peace and reconciliation are rapidly having our credibility eroded since, as we speak, your side replies with police dogs, with teargas, with bullets, and with death. That way lies the destruction of all of us, black and white together. Come, let us walk tall together into the wonderful future that can be ours, black and white together, a wonderful future for our children, black and white together. Don't wait until it is too late; don't wait until we have the fulfillment of the ghastly prophecy in *Cry, the Beloved Country*[2]—"when they are turned to loving, they will find we are turned to hating." Please hear us before it is too late.

2

Early in 1979 Tutu addressed a service in Regina Mundi Catholic Church, Soweto, an important venue for protest rallies by young activists, which commemorated the victims of the Sharpeville Massacre in 1960. The Sharpeville killings, in which police shot dead more than seventy people demonstrating against apartheid laws, started a chain of events—including the declaration of a state of emergency, the banning of liberation movements, such movements' resort to armed struggle, and the jailing of Nelson Mandela and other leaders—that ended in the suppression of militant action against apartheid for a decade. With their uprising in Soweto in 1976, the young people to whom Tutu addressed the following words at Regina Mundi early in 1979 had brought this era to an end.

I stand before you as a bishop in the one holy catholic and apostolic church of God, and therefore I stand before you as a Christian leader. I want to stress this to you today, my friends, because we are accused so often of dragging politics into religion. I stand before you today as someone who has tried, and continues to try, to be faithful toward our Lord and Master Jesus Christ. I stand before you as one who claims that what I say and do is not dictated and determined by my political philosophy. I stand before you today as someone who has no political affiliations. I stand before you today as someone who declares that he has no political ambitions. I stand before you today to declare that I don't see myself as an Archbishop Makarios, who was president of Cyprus, nor as a Bishop Abel Muzorewa.[3]

I stand before you today to declare that it is not my politics but my faith that determines what I do or say. It is my commitment and my obedience to our Lord Jesus Christ which determines what I do or say. I know that if Bishop Tutu were to say today that he thinks that apartheid or this system of separate development[4] or whatever it is called, if I were to say that this system is not bad, do you know that, wonderfully, nobody would accuse me of dragging politics into religion? It is a thing that is somewhat odd, isn't it, that whenever one declares an unjust and oppressive system to be evil and unrighteous, *then* one is said to bring politics into religion?

We declare that the God whom we worship is the Lord of all life, not just of parts of life—those that are called "religious" or "sacred." What about economics, what about politics? Do we want to say that our God does not care about these? I am sorry, but that is not what the Bible says. Listen to this passage from the prophet Isaiah:

> *Why have we fasted, and thou seest it not?*
> *Why have we humbled ourselves, and thou takest no*
> *   knowledge of it?*
> *Behold, in the day of your fast you seek your own pleasure,*
> *and oppress all your workers.*
> *Behold, you fast only to quarrel and to fight*
> *and to hit with wicked fist.*
> *Fasting like yours this day*
> *will not make your voice to be heard on high.*
> *Is such the fast that I choose,*

a day for a man to humble himself?
Is it to bow down his head like a rush,
and to spread sackcloth and ashes under him?
Will you call this a fast,
and a day acceptable to the Lord?
Is not this the fast that I choose:
to loose the bonds of wickedness,
to undo the thongs of the yoke,
to let the oppressed go free,
and to break every yoke?
Is it not to share your bread with the hungry,
and bring the homeless poor into your house;
when you see the naked, to cover him,
and not to hide yourself from your own flesh?
Then shall your light break forth like the dawn,
and your healing shall spring up speedily;
your righteousness shall go before you,
the glory of the Lord shall be your rear guard.

ISAIAH 58:3–8, RSV

Isaiah is condemning religious practices if these have no bearing and relevance to the social, political, and economic sphere. He is saying that such religion is an insult to God and therefore blasphemous. It is as if religious people were trying to bribe God. "God, we will do this for you if you let us do as we please." God says, "Not on your life." We know, too, that when Jesus, the very Son of God himself, walked this earth, he did not say to sick people, "Never mind: things will be all right for you in heaven." No, he healed the sick; he opened the eyes of the blind; he fed the hungry. Anybody who tries today to tell people who are oppressed, who live in slums and hovels, who are shunted about from one place to another, who are evicted from their homes and made to sleep in tents on pavements because they are the wrong skin color, who are paid low wages as cheap labor, who live in matchbox houses with inadequate lighting and unpaved streets and inadequate recreation facilities, who must get up at four A.M. in order to be at work at seven or eight because the transport system is inadequate, who can't educate their children because they must pay for that education while the rich ones of this land can have their children educated freely and compulsorily—if anyone can tell people in those conditions not to worry because things will be all right in heaven, then such a person makes a mockery of the religion of Jesus Christ.

In the story Jesus Christ told about the Last Judgment, he says that we determine whether we are fit for heaven or hell by whether or not we have done certain things. In the list that he gives, nowhere does he say, "You'll go to heaven just because you prayed or because you went to church." Now, don't say I said that he did not think these things were important, but it is significant that he does not mention them—he mentions feeding the hungry, clothing the naked, visiting the sick and those in prison. How many people banned by the government have you visited? How many times have you attended political trials? Jesus Christ says that you can't love

God whom you have not seen unless you love your brother whom you know and see, because he says, "Love the Lord thy God with all thy heart . . . and thy neighbor as thyself" (Luke 10:27, KJV). It is my relationship with Jesus Christ and with God which compels me to be involved in politics, in economics, in the struggle for liberation of our people; and nobody, I'm afraid, can change that, because for me that is what it means to be a Christian in South Africa today.

Nineteen years ago our people protested peacefully at Sharpeville against the pass laws.[5] Nineteen years ago! What has happened since then? Well, we are told that things are changing in South Africa. Don't make me laugh! Things are changing indeed! We used to be harassed nineteen years ago by the police for passes and we used to see our fathers and brothers handcuffed, in a "crocodile," being paraded down the streets. Today, the police have stepped up the pass raids. Last year there was an increase of a hundred thousand in the number of people arrested. There is no change, certainly not for the better. Any change is for the worse. Our people are being arrested so that people will not see just how many blacks are unemployed. They are dumped not as human beings, but as superfluous appendages—that is what a cabinet minister once called them—in the Bantustans. Out of sight is then out of mind.

With all the authority I have as a Christian leader and with all the passion I can command as a human being, I want to make this appeal and to issue this warning. The actions of the police are highly provocative. Stop them, please; otherwise one day we will have a serious outburst. We are human beings with feelings too.

We are human beings created by God. We have dignity. Don't go on like this—humiliating us daily. Don't make us desperate, for even the worm will turn, as they say. And desperate people will use desperate means.

I call on our white fellow South Africans. These things are done in your name. Repudiate them if you want to have a future you can be proud of in a nonracial South Africa. Don't be deluded: black people will one day have political power in this country. Nobody and nothing will stop that happening. So side with those who are winning.

Our struggle is a just struggle. Our struggle is a moral struggle, and for that reason it is bound to succeed. White people know they are supporting an unjust, oppressive, and evil system. God can't be mocked. He is a God of justice and goodness and love—and he is on our side, because we are oppressed. He will defeat evil and injustice. He wants all his children, black and white, to be free. We want a nonracial South Africa where all black and white will count, not because of the color of their skin, but because all black and white have been created in God's image.

> *What then shall we say to this? If God is for us, who is against us?*
> *He who did not spare his own Son but gave him up for us all, will he not also give us all things with him?*
> *Who shall bring any charge against God's elect? It is God who justifies; who is to condemn? Is it Christ Jesus, who died, yes, who was raised from the dead, who is at the right hand of God, who indeed intercedes for us?*

Who shall separate us from the love of Christ? Shall tribulation, or distress, or persecution, or famine, or nakedness, or peril, or sword?

As it is written, "For your sake we are being killed all the day long; we are regarded as sheep to be slaughtered."

No, in all these things we are more than conquerors through him who loved us.

For I am sure that neither death, nor life, nor angels, nor principalities, nor things present, nor things to come, nor powers, nor height, nor depth, nor anything else in all creation, will be able to separate us from the love of God in Christ Jesus our Lord.

ROMANS 8:31–39, RSV

CHAPTER 12

Utterly Diabolical

Appeal to the Morality of a Fellow Christian

*Apartheid turned black South Africans into units of labor, tolerated
in the industrial and agricultural heartland of the country for only as
long as they served the white-run economy and constantly subject to
deportation to rural, ethnically based enclaves (called "Bantustans"
or "homelands") in which the black majority were meant to exercise
their political rights. After taking power in 1948, the architects of
apartheid began, in their drive to enforce racial and ethnic purity,
to shunt people around the country, moving blacks living in areas
deemed too close to white suburbs to new locations outside the cities,
or forcing them into the particular Bantustans created for their
supposed ethnic groups. According to a 1978 estimate, the government had forcibly removed 2.1 million people from their homes and
still planned to move another 1.7 million. Observing the effects of
the removals precipitated Desmond Tutu's initial major confrontation with the government. He had first become known in the white*

community by warning—in a newspaper editorial and in a widely
publicized open letter to Prime Minister B. J. Vorster six weeks before
the Soweto uprising—of his "growing nightmarish fear" of "bloody
confrontation" if apartheid was not abandoned. Three years later, he
wrote another letter—unpublicized for more than three decades—to
Vorster's successor, P. W. Botha, who upon taking office had suggested
that he was willing to consider introducing limited reforms to meet
the needs of white business.

The Hon. the Prime Minister
Mr. P. W. Botha
Private Bag X193
Cape Town, 8000

5 July 1979

Dear Mr. Prime Minister,

Re: POPULATION RESETTLEMENT SCHEMES

I write to you as one South African leader to another, as one
South African to a fellow South African. But more fundamentally
I write to you as one Christian to his fellow Christian. I write to you
confidently because you have been very forthcoming and courteous
in the correspondence we have had so far on other matters.

I write confidently about this subject which since last week has become almost obsessional with me because I believe that you are unaware of the conditions that shattered me during my visit to the Eastern Cape. I am convinced that if you knew what the consequences of the massive population resettlement schemes have been on your fellow human beings and your fellow South Africans, then you and your colleagues in the Nationalist Party would long ago have called a halt to something with such distressing results.

I write confidently because I am sure that you are attempting to steer this country from the politics of confrontation to those of dialogue and coexistence. And I accept your bona fides in this regard. I believe you do want to usher in a new dispensation but have to move circumspectly because many believe that there could very well be a right-wing backlash. It is irrelevant at this point to say that I think that this is a grossly exaggerated fear despite recent by-election indications about an apparent upsurge in support for the HNP.[1] I myself believe that the white community in our beloved land longs to follow you into a future whose security is assured not primarily through police and military power but because all the inhabitants of our beloved motherland recognize that they have a stake in things. And they look to you to demonstrate in reality that apartheid is indeed moribund if not quite dead yet.[2]

I write to you to say that the policy of population removal and resettlement is quite indefensible on moral and pragmatic grounds. People who have been working perhaps full-time or as

casual laborers are resettled a long distance from possible points of
employment. They used to have adequate accommodation in their
former homes and then they are dumped in some God-forsaken
place where often no adequate alternative accommodation and
services have been provided. This is wantonly wasteful. They
end up workless, frustrated, and starving. Funds have to be
found to re-house them in some fashion or other while there is
already a serious housing shortage and all available resources for
this ought to be invested in decreasing this backlog.

But it is the moral aspect that has shattered me and that I
believe you and your colleagues must be unaware of. And it is
that human persons are treated as if they are less than that. I
must be careful not to use emotive language, but Mr. Prime
Minister, I cannot avoid speaking about the dumping of people
as if they were things, with little prior consultation about how
they felt about things and almost certainly scant attention
being paid to how they feel. I cannot see how such treatment is
consistent with the gospel of Jesus Christ, who said, "Inasmuch
as you did not do it to the least of these my brethren, you did not
do it unto me" (Matthew 25:45).

I am trying to be as restrained as possible because I want to
confess to you that at this moment as I write I am deeply agitated
and angered by what I have seen. I know that a former cabinet
minister spoke of our mothers and fathers when they could no
longer be of use to the whites as "superfluous appendages." We
have not forgotten this appellation—that excess blacks in so-
called white South Africa would be moved into rural areas to

be out of sight and out of mind as some people thought, so that they and others would be part of a reservoir of cheap black labor under the migratory labor system.

I do not think you know what government policy has done and is doing to persons created by God, the Father, redeemed by Jesus Christ, and sanctified by God the Holy Spirit. I do not think you know that women sweep the streets of Sada for R6[3] per month, where their rent has doubled from R1 per room per month to R2 and if you have three rooms then your monthly wage all goes to pay that increased rent. I do not think you know that an old man in Glenmore could earn R2.50 a day near his old home and now must pay R6.50 for the return journey to the same place. If he can work for four days, of his R10 wages more than 50 percent is now to be used up in bus fares. I do not think you know of the little girl in Zweledinga who said she and her mother and sister lived on borrowed food, and if they could not borrow food they drank water to fill their stomachs—this in a country that exports food. No Sir, I do not think you know any of this, because I am sure your Christian conscience would hardly permit you to support anything so evil as its consequences for the children of God. You would call an immediate halt to these resettlement schemes.

You and Dr. Koornhof[4] courageously stopped the demolition of Crossroads in Cape Town and Alexandra Township in Johannesburg. I appeal to you in the name of our Lord Jesus Christ, please stop any further removals of blacks today; then people would believe there was more than rhetoric in the ministerial proclamations about the death of apartheid. I myself will always be haunted by that little girl, and I pledge myself to do all I can to see an end to what I believe to be utterly diabolical and unacceptable to the Christian conscience. I have no doubt whatsoever that once you realize what these removals mean, you will share my sense of urgency and passion to have them stopped immediately.

We want justice, peace, and reconciliation in our land, and these will come as we strive to remove all which makes people less than what God intends them to be. We will be free together or not at all.

I pray that God will have given me the words to convey the anguish of so many to you and that he will give you grace and strength to stop these resettlement schemes. The Afrikaner has found it difficult to forget the concentration camps in which some of his forebears were incarcerated by the British.[5] Black memories of the resettlement camps and villages may be equally indelible. This is an urgent and serious matter, and I request that even in your very busy schedule you will please respond to my plea at your earliest convenience.

The evangelist St. John calls passionately to all of us: "My children, our love should not be just words and talk; it must be true love which shows itself in action." Later he appeals to us in these words: "Dear friends, let us love one another, because love comes from God. Whoever loves is a child of God and knows God. Whoever does not love does not know God, for God is love." Earlier the same St. John asks us all: "If a rich person sees his brother in need, yet closes his heart against his brother, how can he claim that he loves God?" (1 John 3:18; 4:7; 3:17, TEV).

Because we are all of us the children of this God, let us behave toward one another as befits our exalted status.

We continue to pray for God's blessing on you and your colleagues, that you may be instruments of his divine gracious will in this beautiful land which we all love so deeply.

Yours sincerely,
Bishop Desmond Tutu
General Secretary
South African Council of Churches

CHAPTER 13

Unbiblical, Unchristian, Immoral, and Evil

When Human Laws Clash with the Law of God

Responding to Desmond Tutu's plea (see previous chapter), Prime Minister Botha acknowledged that black South Africans were being relocated but said that it was not government policy to "dump" people. "Although it is conceded that the removal of people from established places of abode may cause inconvenience in some cases," Botha said, "the ultimate advantages far outweigh the initial disadvantages." Despite the rejection, Tutu tried again repeatedly to engage Botha in meaningful dialogue. He was unsuccessful, and confrontation between the churches and the state grew steadily, intensifying particularly after the nation's final, and ultimately successful, internal rebellion against apartheid began in 1984.

1

Early in 1987 police issued an order under state-of-emergency regulations prohibiting public participation in any campaign calling for the release of detainees, which made it illegal for churches to hold services to pray for the release of people held without trial. The police backed down in the face of church protests, but not before a service had been called, for which Tutu prepared this response.

In this service we are going to pray for those in detention without trial, to ask God to strengthen them in their time of desolation, and we will urge the authorities to release these detainees or to bring them to trial before an open court.

Now those are fairly innocuous actions, and they were happening fairly frequently in this country without any trouble and with no one getting into trouble for carrying them out. That was until last Friday, when the commissioner of police gazetted a set of restrictions which seemed to make such activity illegal under the provisions of the state of emergency. Now I want to assure you, in case you might have been led to think otherwise, that you are not behind the Iron Curtain or in some other totalitarian police state or in Nazi Germany, where such restrictions would be par for the course. We are holding a service for detainees, which was deemed illegal in the Republic of South Africa—a country whose latest constitution, 1984 model, in its preamble actually invokes the name of God. The authorities would say that they are themselves Christians who are determined to uphold what are usually claimed to be Western Christian standards and ideals, and they would say that South Africa belongs in the family of Western nations.

This country claims that among the standards and institutions of Western civilization that it upholds is freedom of worship and freedom of religion. The provisions of the latest restrictions are an intolerable and quite unacceptable abrogation of that freedom and the rule of law. Many of our churches include in their normal intercessions prayers for detainees and their families, and they will often have someone or other who is affected intimately by this state of emergency. And the congregation will show solidarity with those who have been so affected. Are all those services to be declared illegal and are the parish magazines which call for prayers and other support for detainees and their relatives to be banned as illegal? It isn't clear whether the services would be construed to be a "gathering" in the meaning of the regulations. Are we showing solidarity with the detainees when we pray as a group, and not as individuals, for their strengthening and their release, for in our church after every petition we say, "Lord in your mercy . . . ," and the congregation replies, "Hear our (not my) prayer."

We believe we have been given a ministry of reconciliation by God himself, to be ambassadors of Christ. In carrying out this ministry, we seek to address those parties involved in strife. We make suggestions about some of the steps which we believe either party should take in order to make reconciliation more likely, to create the appropriate climate for negotiation. So we go to speak with the ANC and make certain proposals which we think will help toward a negotiated settlement of the serious crisis of our beloved country. It is in this light that the calls of our own church and that of others should be seen, where we say that the irreducible minimum conditions for creating a climate conducive to negotiation would be lifting the state of emergency, releasing political prisoners and detainees, unbanning black political organizations, and then talking to the authentic leaders and representatives of every section of our society. We believe it is part of carrying out a divine mandate given to us to do this. And now the government, claiming to be Christian, wants to prescribe to us just how we should carry out our God-given work.

A government has the obligation to see that persons enjoy their rights in such a way that they do not infringe on those of others, also that they do not lead to an undermining of a legitimate social order that meets with the concurrence of the majority of those who are ruled. No one in their right mind could ever claim that calls for the release of detainees fall into that category. Can anyone explain how calling for the unbanning of black political organizations by groups should not be regarded as subversive while appealing for the release of detainees should be so regarded? It makes us inhabitants of an Alice-in-Wonderland world. No one in their right mind could ever construe nonviolent appeals, petitions, telegrams, and even campaigns for the release of detainees as subversive—in fact, they would say it was working for a more just dispensation.

The authorities want to arrogate to themselves a right that can belong only to God, and when a clash occurs between the laws of man and the laws of God, then for the Christian there can be no debate or argument about which he must obey. Our Lord told those

who questioned him, "Render unto Caesar the things that belong
to Caesar and render unto God the things that belong to God"
(Matthew 22:21). Caesar can never be God. He is God's servant,
to ensure that good and just order prevails. Caesar cannot claim
absolute authority without becoming blasphemous. And the latest
government orders are blasphemous. Christians cannot obey them
without dishonoring God in giving to man that which belongs by
right to God. We had much rather obey God than man, as the
apostles told the Sanhedrin, the Jewish council. We are normally
law-abiding people, but when the honor of God is at stake, then we
will disobey thoroughly iniquitous and unjust laws.

Please let us be mindful of the important distinction between
what is legal and what is morally right. The latest draconian emergency regulations are legal, but without doubt they are immoral
and totalitarian. They belong in a police state. My father was fond
of quoting to me the saying, "Those whom the gods would destroy
they first make mad." I think the authorities in this latest orgy of
restrictions have seemingly gone out of their minds. Their unre-
stricted power has gone to their heads. Power, they say, tends to
corrupt, and absolute power tends to corrupt absolutely.

I am black, and there are many times when I have asked whether
God really cared for blacks when I have looked at some of the
things that our people have suffered. When the South African Defence Force raided Maputo and Maseru a few years ago,[1] we were
told we could not hold memorial services. I held such services because I did not think then nor do I think now that I can be told by
a secular authority what services I may or may not hold. They kill

our children and then prescribe how we may bury them, and they think we do not hurt. What do they think happens to us?

For the government, we are really less than human, spoken of as "those people." Our pain, our anguish one day will burst forth in an unstoppable flood. Please don't do it to us. Now we are being told that we must not even appeal for the release of our children, eleven-year-olds held in detention—that to do so would be subversive. Surely what is subversive is the political system that makes such abominable practices possible. Will the authorities arrest a mother who pleads publicly, "Please release my child"? If a family meets together and calls for the release of a brother, a son, etc., will that family be arrested? If a group of mothers whose children are detained get together and cry from their hearts, "Please release our children," will they be sentenced to ten days' imprisonment or fines of R20,000? If they wear shirts saying, "Please bring my child back," will they be arrested?

I am determined not just to make a call for the release of detainees but to move others to realize how utterly scandalous and outrageous it is for children, for instance, to be held in detention. And to urge Christians in our church certainly to condemn such an unjust system and to do all they can to let the authorities know their opposition to it. If we can no longer peacefully campaign for change in an evil and unjust system, is the government saying then that the only alternative is violence? What else will be left for people to do? Is the government saying virtually all peaceful protest is now forbidden? Let them not play semantic games with convoluted regulations which seem to confuse even eminent lawyers about their import.

Friends, the leaders of our government have gone crazy. Maybe they did not know what they were really doing. Let me tell them something. I am not going to stop calling for the release of detainees in church and outside church, in a service or a gathering, because I believe it is part of my vocation as a Christian. And whatever the consequences, I urge the authorities to release all detainees or to bring them to court immediately, and I hope you support me in such a call. Should the authorities arrest and charge me, when I return, I will again call for the release of detainees if there are still any around. I will urge my congregations and others to be engaged in a campaign to do so peacefully and nonviolently, whatever the consequences for me.

Let me warn the government yet again, as I did when Mr. Louis le Grange, Mr. Adriaan Vlok's predecessor in office as the police minister, made unfounded accusations against the South African Council of Churches when I was its general secretary: you are not God. You may be powerful, perhaps even very powerful, but you are not God. You are mere mortals. Beware when you take on the church of God. Others have tried it before, and they came a cropper. They bit the dust and did so ignominiously—the Roman Emperor Nero, Hitler, Amin, and many others. You will end up being part of the flotsam and jetsam of history, hardly a footnote on the pages of history.

Please hear our cry. Get rid of the monster of your creating, apartheid, and we will have a new South Africa—just, nonracial, and democratic, where black and white will exist side by side amicably together in their home country as members of one family, the human family, God's family.

2

In February 1988, after the government had introduced further restrictions on the activities of political organizations, church leaders gathered in Cape Town and defied a ban on public protest to lead a march of clergy to deliver a petition to Parliament. In the stormy weeks that followed, Cape Town community leaders formed a new ad hoc committee to act in place of the organizations that had been restricted, the government banned that committee, the community leaders called a protest rally at a university campus, and the government banned the rally. Tutu responded by calling for a service in St. George's Cathedral on the same day and at the same time as the rally had been advertised. Addressing a multifaith congregation with the following words, he struck a note of defiance.

We are gathered today to pray for our country, which faces a deepening crisis, to reflect on what is taking place and our role as believers—as Christians, as Muslims, as Jews, whatever. What would be our role in this crisis? In the enveloping darkness, as the lights of freedom are extinguished one by one, despite all the evidence to the contrary, we have come here to say that evil, and injustice, and oppression, and exploitation—embodied in the very essence, the very nature, of apartheid—cannot prevail.

In the Bible, we are told to speak to spiritual things. St. John says, "The light shineth in the darkness, and the darkness did not overwhelm the light" (John 1:5). We come to sustain our hope that this is so. Humanly speaking, as we look around at our situation, that situation appears hopeless. But we must assert, and assert confidently, that this is God's world, that God is in charge.

We must say to our rulers, especially unjust rulers such as those in this land: "You may be powerful—indeed, very powerful—but you are not God. You are ordinary mortals! God—the God whom we worship—can't be mocked. You have already lost! You have already lost! Let us say to you nicely, You have already lost; we are inviting you to come and join the winning side. Come! Come and join the winning side. Your cause is unjust. You are defending what is fundamentally indefensible, because it is evil. It is evil without question. It is immoral. It is immoral without question. It is unchristian. Therefore, you will bite the dust! And you will bite the dust comprehensively!"

3

Ten days later, under pressure from British Prime Minister Margaret Thatcher and United States Secretary of State George Shultz, Botha agreed to meet with Tutu to hear a plea for amnesty for six people about to be hanged for taking part in the mob killing of a local official in Sharpeville in 1984. Infuriated by the open civil disobedience of the heads of the country's most prominent churches, Botha used the meeting—and a letter he handed to Tutu responding to the petition—to berate the archbishop for leading an illegal march and accuse him of being part of an ANC and South African Communist Party campaign to establish "an atheistic Marxist state." Below are excerpts from Tutu's reply to that letter.

I want to state quite categorically that I stand by all that I have done and said in the past concerning the application of the gospel of Jesus Christ to the situation of injustice and oppression and exploitation, which are of the very essence of apartheid, a policy which your government has carried out with ruthless efficiency. My position in this matter is not one of which I am ashamed or for which I would ever want to apologize. I know that I stand in the mainline Christian tradition. My theological position derives from the Bible and from the teaching of the church. The Bible and the church predate Marxism and the ANC by several centuries.

May I give you a few illustrations? The Bible teaches that what invests each person with infinite value is not this or that arbitrarily chosen biological attribute, but the fact that each person is created in the image of God (Genesis 1:26). Apartheid, the policy of your government, claims that what makes a person qualify for privilege and political power is that biological irrelevance, the color of a person's skin and his ethnic antecedents. Apartheid says those are what make a person matter. That is clearly at variance with the teaching of the Bible and the teaching of our Lord and Savior Jesus Christ. Hence the church's criticism that your apartheid policies are not only unjust and oppressive; they are positively unbiblical, unchristian, immoral, and evil.

Apartheid has said that ultimately people are intended for separation. You have carried out policies enshrined in the Population Registration Act, the Group Areas Act, segregated education, health, etc. The Bible teaches quite unequivocally that people are created for fellowship, for togetherness, not for alienation, apartness, enmity, and division (Genesis 2:18; Genesis 11:1–9; Acts 17:26; Romans 12:3–5; 1 Corinthians 12:12–13; Galatians 3:28).

I could show that apartheid teaches the fundamental irreconcilability of people because they belong to different races. This is at variance with the central teaching of the Christian faith about the reconciling work of our Lord and Savior Jesus Christ. "God was in Christ reconciling the world to himself," declares St. Paul (2 Corinthians 5:19, REB), summing up teaching contained in other parts of the New Testament (John 12:32, Ephesians 1:10; Ephesians 2:14, etc.). I could show that in dealing with human beings as if they were less than those who are created in the image of God and by inflicting untold and unnecessary suffering on them, as through your vicious policies of forced population removals, you have contravened basic ethical tenets. I could provide further evidence that your apartheid policies are unbiblical, unchristian, immoral, and evil. It is for these and other reasons that our church and other churches have declared apartheid a heresy.

What we are doing is no innovation when we bring the Word of God as we understand it to bear on the situation in which we are involved. The prophets of old, when they declared, "Thus saith the Lord . . ." to the rulers and the powerful of their day, were our forerunners. They spoke about the need for religion to show its authenticity by how it affected the everyday life of the people, and especially by how the rich, the powerful, the privileged, and the rulers dealt with the less privileged, the poor, the hungry, the oppressed, the widow, the orphan, and the alien.

Isaiah said God rejected all religious observances, however punc-
tilious and elaborate. He urged worshippers:

> *Put away the evil of your deeds, away out of my sight.*
> *Cease to do evil and learn to do right, pursue justice*
> *and champion the oppressed; give the orphan his rights,*
> *plead the widow's cause.*
>
> ISAIAH 1:16–17, NEB

Elsewhere he claimed that God was not pleased with their religious fasts. God declared through the prophet:

> *Is not this what I require of you as a fast:*
> *to loose the fetters of injustice,*
> *to untie the knots of the yoke,*
> *to snap every yoke*
> *and set free those who have been crushed?*
> *Is it not sharing your food with the hungry,*
> *taking the homeless poor into your house,*
> *clothing the naked when you meet them*
> *and never evading a duty to your kinsfolk?*
>
> ISAIAH 58:6–7, NEB

Elijah confronted the king about his injustice to Naboth, a nonentity as far as the king was concerned, but a man who was championed by God (1 Kings: 21); Nathan was not afraid to convict David of his sinfulness (2 Samuel: 12). This kind of involvement of religion with politics and the habit of religious leaders to speak into the sociopolitical and economic situation can be attested to as standard practice in the Bible, which provides our mandate and paradigm.

Our marching orders come from Christ himself and not from any human being. Our mandate is provided by the Bible and the teaching of the church, not by any political group or ideology, Marxist or otherwise.

Our Lord himself adopted as a description of his program that which was outlined by Isaiah:

> *The spirit of the Lord God is upon me*
> *because the Lord has anointed me;*
> *he has sent me to bring good news to the humble,*
> *to bind up the broken-hearted,*
> *to proclaim liberty to captives*
> *and release to those in prison;*
> *to proclaim a year of the Lord's favor*
> *and a day of the vengeance of our God.*
>
> ISAIAH 61:1–2, NEB

Jesus quotes this in his first sermon as recorded by St. Luke (Luke 4:16–21). He stood in the prophetic tradition when he taught what criteria would be used to judge the nations—it would be not through observance of narrowly defined religious duties but by whether they had fed the hungry, clothed the naked, visited the sick and imprisoned, etc. (Matthew 25:31–46).

We are law-abiding. Good laws make human society possible. When laws are unjust, then Christian tradition teaches that they do not oblige obedience. Our Lord broke not just man's law but, what was considered more serious, he broke God's law in order to meet human need—as when he broke the law of the Sabbath observance (John 5:8–14). He paid due regard to the secular ruler in the person of Pontius Pilate but subsequently engaged in a defiance of that secular authority when he refused to answer Pilate's questions (Mark 15:3–5).

It is a hallowed tradition of direct nonviolent action such as we engaged in when we tried to process to Parliament. We were mindful too of what the apostles said to the Jewish Sanhedrin: that obedience to God takes precedence over obedience to human beings (Acts 4:19, 5:29).

We accept wholeheartedly St. Paul's teaching in Romans 13—that we should submit ourselves to earthly rulers (vv. 1–2). Their authority is not absolute, however. They themselves also stand under God's judgment as his servants. They are meant to instill fear only in those who do wrong, holding no terror for those who do right (Romans 13:3). The ruler is God's servant to do the subjects good (Romans 13:4). The ruler rules for the benefit of the ruled. That comes not out of a political manifesto but from the holy scriptures. The corollary is that you must not submit yourself to a ruler who subverts your good. That is why we admire those who oppose unjust regimes—for example, totalitarian Communist governments. The Bible teaches that governments can become beasts in the symbolic language of the book of Revelation (Revelation 13). Not too many governments nor their apologists who use Romans 13 with glee are quite so enthusiastic about its full implications.

I want to state the obvious—that I am a Christian religious leader. By definition that surely means I reject Communism and Marxism as atheistic and materialistic. I try to work for the extension of the kingdom of God, which will ultimately have rulers such as the ones described in Isaiah 11:1–9 and in Psalm 72:1–4 and 12–14:

> *O God, endow the king with thy own justice,*
> *and give thy righteousness to a king's son,*
> *that he may judge thy people rightly*
> *and deal out justice to the poor and suffering.*
> *May hills and mountains afford thy people*
> *peace and prosperity in righteousness.*
> *He shall give judgment for the suffering*
> *and help those of the people that are needy;*
> *he shall crush the oppressor. . . .*
> *For he shall rescue the needy from their rich oppressors,*
> *the distressed who have no protector.*
> *May he have pity on the needy and the poor,*

deliver the poor from death;
may he redeem them from oppression and violence
and may their blood be precious in his eyes.

PSALM 72:1–4, 12–14, NEB

I work for God's kingdom. For whose kingdom with your apartheid policy do you work? I pray for you, as I do for your ministerial colleagues, every day by name.

PART FOUR

South Africa's Conscience

CHAPTER 14

We Must Turn the Spotlight on Ourselves

On Hatred, Revenge, and the Culture of Violence

Under apartheid, Tutu saw himself as an "interim leader" in the political arena, providing direction only because many other leaders were in prison, in exile, or under house arrest. After Botha's successor, F. W. de Klerk, unbanned liberation movements and released Nelson Mandela and other leaders from prison in February 1990, Tutu assumed a stance of "critical solidarity" toward them, supporting their demands for democracy but reserving the right to criticize them. As power began to shift toward the liberation movements during negotiations on a democratic constitution, old patterns of influence and privilege crumbled, leading to instability and intracommunal violence in black communities, fomented by elements within the apartheid government fighting to retain power.

1

In September 1990 Tutu and his bishops made a pastoral visit to Sebokeng, south of Johannesburg, a community that was in turmoil after more than thirty people had been killed in attacks by vigilantes armed by apartheid counterinsurgency units. In stops at the scene of the killings, in the local church, and where crowds of angry young people gathered in the streets, Tutu urged calm.

Now, my brothers and sisters, my dear children, let us not allow the enemy to divide us. The enemy is doing everything it can to divide us. We must not allow the enemy to come between us! Let us not allow the enemy to fill us with hatred! We are hurt; yes, we are hurt. But we have come here to try to pour oil on your hurt. Know that your hurts are our hurts. You are not suffering alone. Your hurts are our hurts. White bishops, black bishops, weep. They weep when they hear of the things that have happened to their children. Your pain is our pain.

But we come here to say, "Children of God, let us show that we are the children of God by not being filled with hatred. Let us not be filled with a desire to revenge." You know they say in the Old Testament that there is a law that says, "An eye for an eye." Okay? Now, Martin Luther King Jr. said something wonderful. He said, "Can you imagine, if we believed in that law of an eye for an eye, very soon all the people would be blind."

We must not allow that to happen. Our freedom is here. Our freedom is here—we are about to touch it—and there are people who are jealous, who say no they don't want us to be free. Don't allow them to take away our prize. Don't allow it. Hold on to one another! Hold on to one another! Say, "We worship a God who we know is a God who leads his people out of bondage into the Promised Land." That is the God we worship. We worship a God who will lead us out of the bondage of apartheid, the bondage of division, lead us into the Promised Land, where black and white and *all* of us will be just one family, God's family.

And we who are Christians have a great privilege; we have the great privilege of saying to people, "Yes, weep, weep, weep for all that has happened, but don't allow hatred." Hatred is like an acid. Once it gets into you, it burns away the skin. Hatred and revenge are like an acid that will eat you, and one day you will discover you are just empty. And so we come here, saying we have no doubt we are going to be free, all of us. Let us say, "We are going to be free!"

2

An estimated fourteen thousand people were killed between Mandela's release and his accession to power in 1994—more than double the number who had died in the final uprising against apartheid. The transition can be likened to a running brawl along the edge of a cliff, the protagonists alternately moving forward, stalling, moving backward, sometimes nearly going off the precipice, but always pulling back from disaster when the nation was most threatened. Tutu became best known in this period for what Mandela called "his inde-

pendent mind," reflected most eloquently in this sermon, preached in
St. George's Cathedral, Cape Town, in 1991.

It seems as if the culture of violence is taking root in our society.
We are becoming brutalized and almost anesthetized to accept
what is totally unacceptable. If this kind of violence that keeps
erupting at regular intervals continues, then the new South Africa
may dawn—and that is doubtful—but it may dawn and there will
be very few around to enjoy it; and those who survive will do so
only because they are tough, on the basis of the laws of the jungle:
survival of the fittest, eat or be eaten, devil take the hindmost.

My friends, yes, there are many reasons why there is violence.

In periods of transition there is the violence due to the instability
of transition, as we have seen in parts of Eastern Europe.

Yes, South Africa has never really had a culture of tolerance. The
government and its supporters have used dastardly and nefarious
methods to deal with their opponents, ranging from the vilification
and pillorying of these, as still happens on SABC-TV and radio
and government-supporting media, up to the physical elimina-
tion of people such as has now been confirmed through the death
squads of such as the CCB.[1] Consequently, people have learned
that those who differ with you are enemies and that the only way
to deal with enemies is to liquidate them.

Yes, that is true.

Some of the violence is due to sociopolitical and economic deprivation, and sociologists will tell you that when you think your life
will end in a cul-de-sac, that you won't make it in the rat race, then

the level of your frustration rises and you break out violently. (See what happened in Britain in those riots against the poll tax. A great deal of the violence was at the hands of whites who felt that they were going to be the left-behinds in the rat race.)

Yes, that is true.

It is true also that we are reaping the horrible harvests of apartheid through the migratory labor system and its ghastly single-sex hostels.[2] It was an explosion waiting to happen, placing virile men in single-sex hostels cheek by jowl with townships where they saw other men leading normal lives with their families. And these hostel-dwellers were alienated from those township communities.

Yes, all that is true.

It is true that the police and the security forces have on the whole behaved disgracefully, being accused on all sides of a lack of professionalism as a peacekeeping force totally unbiased, and sometimes it might be true that some of them have sought to foment the violence.

Yes, that has added fuel to the fire.

Yes, that is all true. But it is not *all* the truth.

A lot of the violence is due to political rivalry. Political groups in the black community are fighting for turf, and they do not seem to know, or certainly some of their followers don't seem to know, that a cardinal tenet of democracy is that people must be free to choose freely whom they want to support. To coerce, to intimidate, is to admit that your policy can't persuade on its own merits. People must be free to choose freely whether they want to participate or not in boycotts, in mass action. That is an irreducible, an incontrovertible aspect of democracy.

Something has gone desperately wrong in the black community. We black people must of course point to all the causes of violence I have pointed out and to others that I have not referred to. But ultimately we must turn the spotlight on ourselves. We can't go on forever blaming apartheid. Of course it is responsible for a great deal of evil. But ultimately, we are human beings, and we have proved it in the resilience we have shown in the struggle for justice. We did not allow ourselves to be demoralized, dehumanized. We could laugh; we could forgive. We refused to be embittered at some of the worst moments in the struggle.

What has gone wrong, that we seem to have lost our reverence for life, when children can dance round someone dying the gruesome death of "necklacing"? Something has gone desperately wrong when our leaders are not listened to by their followers. There is much to admire in our political organizations, but there is much also which is not right. Some of those who belong to these organizations are totally undisciplined, and you can't wage a struggle unless you are dedicated and disciplined. Our organizations need to go back to the grass roots and instill discipline from the lowest ranks up.

It seems to me that we in the black community have lost our sense of *ubuntu*—our humaneness, caring, hospitality, our sense of connectedness, our sense that my humanity is bound up in your humanity. We are losing our self-respect, demonstrated it seems to me most graphically by the horrible extent of dumping and littering in our townships. Of course we live in squalor and in slum ghettos. But we are not rubbish. Why do we seem to *say* that is what we are when you see how we treat our already poor environment?

There are some things that I want to suggest we can do.

The first is that all of us must help to develop the culture of tolerance: live and let live. Let us practice the motto: I disagree with what you say, but I will defend to the death your right to say it. Let us learn to agree to disagree. Those who disagree with us are not necessarily enemies; otherwise there would be very few husbands and wives around!

Second, our political organizations need to put their houses in order; to instill discipline in their members; to adopt at least a minimum code of conduct that says, These are the parameters beyond which we will not stray in conducting our political activity.

Third, the authorities must disarm all groups. It is nonsensical, utterly unacceptable, to speak about "traditional weapons."[3] Traditional weapons kill. And it is quite wrong to allow certain groups blatantly to move around armed.

Fourth, let the police become a truly professional peacekeeping force that upholds the rule of law and order without fear or favor. And one hopes that they can begin to be flexible. For what happened in Daveyton—the killing of eighteen people there—was due to their insisting on the observance of a law that many of our people refuse to obey, that relates to meetings and demonstrations.[4]

Fifth, I urge that all political leaders stop their killing-talk; stop their belligerent, bellicose utterances that incite others to violence, whatever the intention of the speaker might have been. There is already legislation available, and I urge the government to use it. Why do they allow people like Dr. Andries Treurnicht[5] to get away with the kind of language that they are using so openly? Can you imagine what would have happened to blacks if they said the kind of things that he has been allowed to say? There is legislation to stop organizations such as the AWB[6] making vilifying, denigratory, insulting, racist remarks that hurt people. The government ought to stamp on such action—and do so firmly and quickly.

Sixth, I want to suggest that the municipalities, city councils, local councils, churches, community organizations, and political groupings participate in a campaign with the people in the townships to clean up those townships. Perhaps our people may then begin to regain a self-esteem, self-respect, and pride that they are losing.

And, with others, finally I suggest that all of us perhaps at midday pause to pray not just for our country, but for all of Africa. There is a simple prayer that many of us use, and I would suggest that it is a prayer that ought to be learned by people everywhere. It is a straightforward prayer, composed by Trevor Huddleston:[7]

> *God bless Africa*
> *Guard her children*
> *Guide her rulers*
> *And give her peace.*

3

Most of those killed during the transition were the residents of poor black neighborhoods, but there were isolated incidents in white middle-

class suburbs as well. In July 1993, gunmen burst into a Sunday
evening service in St. James Church, Cape Town, and attacked the
multiracial congregation with automatic rifles and hand grenades,
killing eleven people. Desmond Tutu addressed an interfaith service
in the Cape Town City Hall during the week after the attack.

Rampant evil is abroad. Evil men perpetrate vile deeds of darkness, of violence, of death, with breathtaking impunity. They have reached the bottom of depravity in attacking and so desecrating a place of divine worship and adoration: God's sanctuary.

A creeping despondency and sense of impotence want to cover our beautiful land like dark, threatening clouds. We must not let that happen. We, the people of Cape Town, say no to that. Let us not let it happen. God will not let it happen.

Our God is a God who is an expert at dealing with evil, with darkness, with death. Out of the darkness and chaos before creation, our God brought into being light, life, goodness, and a created order which, when he beheld it, he declared to be "very good."

And out of the despair, the evil, the darkness, the pain of slavery, God, our God, brought about the great deliverance, the Exodus. God, our God, created out of a rabble of disorganized slaves his own special people, whom God led out of bondage into the Promised Land, because God, our God, is a God of freedom. Our God is a God of justice, of peace and goodness.

Supremely, God, our God, did his stuff in the awfulness of the cross—its violence, its darkness, and its death. For out of this ghastly instrument of death and destruction, our God produced the glorious victory of Jesus Christ in the resurrection—a victory that was victory of life over death, of light over darkness, of goodness over evil. And you and I must grasp that fact, that we have a God of victory—as the chorus says, "What a mighty God we have!"

We used to say in the darkness of repression, in the most awful times of apartheid's suppression, *"Moenie worry, alles sal regkom."* [Don't worry, everything will turn out all right.] Because our God is a God who will bring justice out of injustice. And they thought we were dreaming. *Nou hier's dit!* [Now here we are!] We are going to have a new South Africa! We are going to have a South Africa where all of us, black and white, will be truly free!

And we, the people of Cape Town today, united in this kind of way against this atrocity, are saying no to violence. To *all* violence! Because we revere each human being. One death is one death too many. We say no to intimidation; we say yes to freedom! We say yes to peace! We say yes to reconciliation!

And we, as we have always said, are the rainbow people of God. We are beautiful because we are the rainbow people of God and we are unstoppable; we are unstoppable, black and white, as we move together to freedom, to justice, to democracy, to peace, to reconciliation, to healing, to loving, to laughter and joy, when we say, "This South Africa belongs to all of us, black and white."

CHAPTER 15

Naught for Your Comfort

A Critique of Comrades and Friends

Within months of Nelson Mandela being sworn in, Desmond Tutu was holding to account South Africa's first democratically elected government, criticizing parliamentarians for voting themselves pay increases and the administration for its failure to close down the apartheid armaments industry. When Mandela hit back by accusing him of being a populist and saying he should raise his concerns privately, Tutu treated the new president like an apartheid cabinet minister: Mandela must be either forgetful or lying, he said, because they had discussed the issues at a private breakfast in the presidential residence in Cape Town. After retiring as archbishop of Cape Town— and chairing the Truth and Reconciliation Commission at Mandela's request—Tutu placed the president's successor, Thabo Mbeki, under similar scrutiny. He was particularly critical of Mbeki's failure to campaign against the devastating spread of HIV and AIDS and to speak out more strongly against the rule in neighboring Zimbabwe of

Robert Mugabe, who relied on the violent suppression of opposition to stay in power. His criticisms were usually couched as single-paragraph interventions in speeches that ranged over other issues. This changed late in 2004, when—early in Mbeki's second term—Tutu delivered two keynote addresses a few months apart. In them, although he gave extensive praise to the ANC government, he also tackled what he identified as disturbing trends, including a US$4 billion military rearmament program, Mbeki's denial of the nature and extent of the HIV and AIDS crisis, and the domination of public life by leaders from South Africa's Nguni language group.[1]

1

This first address was an inaugural lecture in honor of Tutu's mentor, Trevor Huddleston, in the Church of Christ the King, Sophiatown, where Tutu had worshipped as a teenager and where Huddleston had served. The lecture series was entitled "Naught for Your Comfort"— from the title of the book by Huddleston which had gained him fame abroad as an anti-apartheid activist.[2] After paying tribute to Huddleston and his religious community, Tutu turned to South Africa in the twenty-first century.

Our skills were honed in the anti-apartheid struggle—as a church we declared that the kingdom of God required a free and democratic South Africa where everyone counted. We were very much in the *against* mode, and apartheid was an obvious enemy out there that galvanized and united us all. Now we have achieved our goal—a free, democratic, nonracial, nonsexist South Africa.

Do you know something? It is a great deal easier to be *against* than to be *for*. I said God was smart to let me retire when we made the transition from repression to democracy, from being in the *against* mode to the *for* mode.

The church is always the agent of the kingdom of God. No political dispensation, however ideal, can be coterminous with that kingdom. There is always a "not yet" aspect. Now the church is no longer the opponent of the government. It must work in solidarity with the government, but it must not be co-opted. It must retain a critical distance so that it can always say, "Thus saith the Lord," without having its patriotism and loyalty to South Africa called into question.

We must commend the government for all the good that it has achieved, and there is much to be thankful for. We have a level of stability, despite all the crime, that is the envy of other lands. Our president is held in high esteem in the councils of the world. What a metamorphosis: for a country that was a universal pariah now to be taking the lead with NEPAD and in the African Union.[3] We are going to host the African Parliament, a huge feather in our cap. The repulsive caterpillar has become the beautiful, attractive butterfly.

You see, we are all fallible, even the best of us. We are all tempted to abuse power, whether in government, civil society—indeed, even in the church. The church should thus be vigilant to call attention to temptations to abuse power, to become corrupt, the temptations of nepotism. We are answerable ultimately to God. We have all left the house of apartheid's bondage. Some, an elite few, have actually crossed the Jordan into the Promised Land. Others, too many, still wallow in the wilderness of degrading, dehumanizing poverty; far too many still live in squalor and deprivation. Much has been done. People have clean water and electricity who never had these before—but we are sitting on a powder keg, because the gap between the rich and the poor is widening, and some of the very rich are now black.

The church must always be there for the poor, the vulnerable, who will always be with us. We cannot, we dare not, wait on government to do everything. It is possible for us to be generous and compassionate. We can share, caring for and sharing with others. Concern for others is the best form of self-interest. Many of us can adopt at least one poor family. We can commit R100 or R200 to one family per month. We can, some of us, adopt a child from a poor family to pay their school fees. Let us do it while we can. We could be overwhelmed by an uprising of the poor, and then we would have nothing to share. Let us put a smile on God's face.

We should be involved in the moral regeneration of our nation. We should recapture the spirit of reverence for human life. Let us stand up against criminals and hijackers, against those involved in white-collar crime. We should seek to fill our people with a love for our land, a pride in our beautiful land, so that we will not pollute and litter. To pollute and litter is a sin and a crime. We should keep all of us on our toes. Only the best is good enough for us, for South Africa.

Apartheid forced the different denominations and indeed the different faith communities to cooperate in the face of a common foe. Now that that foe has been vanquished, we have tended to retreat into our denominational ghettos and are no longer as keen as formerly to engage in interfaith dialogue and cooperation. The developments in the Middle East have affected especially the relations between Muslim and Jew to the detriment of our land. We should be keen to promote interchurch and interfaith dialogue and cooperation.

A distressing phenomenon in our country is the rise of xenophobia. Understandably, locals may resent competition for such scarce commodities as jobs and accommodation, but that competition can never justify xenophobia. Can we have forgotten so soon just how other African countries bore the brunt of cross-border hot-pursuit attacks by the South African Defence Force? Can we have forgotten how poor countries gave refuge and asylum to our exiles and accommodated our liberation movements at very great cost to themselves? We as the church must speak out against this evil. Yes, of course some of these asylum seekers and refugees may be criminals and drug dealers, but surely we know how painful it is to suffer under stereotypes. Not all Nigerians are drug peddlers.[4]

When I chaired the Truth and Reconciliation Commission, I was appalled by a certain phenomenon. It did seem as if Ngunis ruled this land. I was Xhosa; the chairs of the Human Rights Commission then, of the Electoral Commission, of the Gender Commission, the then public protector, and the national director of prosecutions were all Nguni. Just count the number of Nguni-speaking people in the cabinet. We need to be very wary. The genocide in Rwanda was because the Tutsi had been top dogs over the Hutu most of the time.[5] Nigeria is shaken by ethnic strife, and it is also behind the atrocities in Darfur in the Sudan, where Arab is pitted so sadly against African. Much of the politics in Kenya is based on tribal affiliation. In Zimbabwe, Ndebele and Shona have tended to belong to different political formations. We should be careful that we are not stoking resentment that could explode one day. South Africa should not become a kind of Nguni-ocracy. We should take seriously half-facetious observations such as "Before I was not white enough; now I am not black enough." Many a truth has been said in jest. We should beware of a simmering resentment that could explode one day.

Yes, it is because we are proud of much that our government has done and is pledged to do that we should hold them to high standards. We must question the appropriateness of spending as much as we are going to on arms. We have no real external enemy. Our real enemies are internal: poverty, crime, disease, and corruption. Those pose a far more serious threat to our land than any external enemy on the horizon.

What is important is to stress that a vibrant democracy is one where vigorous debate, dissent, disagreement, and discussion are welcomed. No one has a monopoly on wisdom and ability. We must avoid kowtowing sycophancy like the plague. If policies are good, then they can withstand scrutiny and dissent. No one is infallible. We must encourage those who ask awkward questions, for our rulers are our rulers because we chose them, and they are accountable to us. We used to say to the apartheid rulers, "You are not God." *No* government can be God. My father liked to say, "Improve your argument; don't raise your voice." Those whom we elected and whom we support should have the self-assurance of being open to scrutiny and debate and especially be able to admit they are wrong when they are.

We should require that our government pursue policies of which we can be proud and which we will be ready to defend stoutly. Our policies toward Zimbabwe are not in that category.

South Africa can be a scintillating success. We are, extraordinarily, even now a symbol of hope for many countries riven by conflict. Our reasonably peaceful transition and our pursuit of forgiveness and reconciliation are inspiring other lands to emulate us. We can, we must, succeed for the sake of God's world; and the church as God's agent must be able to say prophetically, "Thus saith the Lord."

2

The Sophiatown lecture (above) attracted little publicity. Three months later, Tutu delivered a nationally broadcast address commemorating the legacy of Nelson Mandela, in which he repeated his praise of the government's successes, then turned to its challenges and failures, focusing more sharply on Mbeki and on the failure of ANC members and leaders to challenge their leader's views.

We are celebrating ten years, a whole decade of freedom, and it is an opportunity for us to look back to assess our achievements and note our failures as we stride into the glorious future opening before us. That is why I have chosen as my title words from the prophet Isaiah: "Look to the rock from which you have been hewn" (Isaiah 51:1, RSV).

What Have We Achieved?

You know that I am repetitive if anything at all. I have been saying that we South Africans tend to sell ourselves short. We seem to be embarrassed with our successes. We have grown quickly blasé, taking for granted some quite remarkable achievements and not giving ourselves enough credit. The result is that we have tended to be despondent, to seem to say that behind every ray of sunshine there must be an invisible cloud—just you wait long enough and it will soon appear. Of course we have problems—serious, indeed devastating problems; but can you please point to any one country in the world today that has no problems? No, I think we should change our perspective. If we are forever looking at our shortcomings and our faults, then the mood will be pervasive and pessimistic, and in a way we will provide the environment that encourages further failure. Don't they say, Give a dog a bad name and hang him? If you have low expectations of people, then don't be surprised if they don't rise above those low expectations. Many people have excelled almost only because someone had faith in them, believed in them, and so inspired them with a new self-belief, a new self-confidence, a new self-esteem. The same is surely true of a nation, which is an aggregate of individuals.

Hey, the world has still not gotten over the fact that we had the reasonably peaceful transition from repression to democracy that we experienced. Have you forgotten so soon how we were on the brink of comprehensive disaster, when most people believed we were going to be overwhelmed by a ghastly racial bloodbath? Have you forgotten so soon what happened during the transition to democracy, when no one could guarantee that if he went off to work in the morning he was going to return alive in the evening, when we had indiscriminate killings on the trains, in the taxis and buses? Do you recall how, when they announced the statistics of the previous twenty-four hours and said six or seven or eight people had been killed, we would often sigh with relief and say, "Well, *only* seven or eight have been killed." Things were in such a desperate state—do you recall the attacks that happened in the hostels? Just think of the massacres that were taking place at regular intervals. There are so very many occasions when it did seem it was touch and go, and none more terrible than the assassination of Chris Hani.[6] That was one of the scariest moments in our lives for most of us. We were a whisker's breadth away from total catastrophe. I said, "If we survived that, we could survive anything." Yes, we did appear to be on the verge of bloody conflagration and disaster. But it did not happen. Instead the world marveled, indeed was awed, by the spectacle of the long, long lines of South Africans of every race snaking their way slowly to the polling booths on that unforgettable, that magical day, April 27, 1994.

We really do have much to celebrate and much for which to be thankful. Hey, just look at us—which other country has a moral colossus to match Nelson Mandela? We are the envy of every single nation on earth. He has become an icon of forgiveness, compassion, magnanimity, and reconciliation for the entire globe. How blessed we are that he was at the helm to guide our ship of state through the choppy waters of transition. We should also salute F. W. de Klerk, who exhibited outstanding moral courage when he announced his breathtaking initiatives on February 2, 1990, that set in motion the process of negotiating a revolution.

Given where we come from, given our antecedents, it is amazing that we should have the stability we enjoy. Russia made the transition from repression to democracy at almost the same time as we did. The Berlin Wall fell in November 1989. Nelson Mandela was released in February 1990. But what is happening in Russia today? The level of Mafia-controlled crime, the conflict with Chechnya—giving such awful examples of carnage as the theater hostage disaster and more recently the Beslan School hostage catastrophe—makes what occurs in South Africa look like a Sunday school picnic.

I often stop to look at the children in the high school near our home in the Cape Town suburb of Milnerton. It used to be an all-white school. Today at breaks you see our demography reflected there. Just a few years ago it was a criminal offense to have that happen. All sorts of dire things, they said, were going to happen if schools were mixed. So far as I can make out, the sky is still firmly in place. You would think that it would be in South Africa where children would have to be escorted by heavily armed police and soldiers to be able to go to school. But no, it isn't in South Africa that that has had to happen; it is in Belfast, Northern Ireland.

Do you recall how police would climb trees in order to peep into bedrooms, hoping to catch out couples who might be contravening the Immorality Act,[7] rushing to feel the temperature of the sheets, making sordid what should have been beautiful—love between two persons—and how many careers and lives were destroyed when people faced charges under this abominable legislation? And now I think I am about the only person who still goggles—look at all those mixed couples who saunter around hand in hand with hardly a care in the world, pushing a pram with a baby of indeterminate hue inside. I still seem to fear that a policeman will come crashing into them for breaking the law. And humiliation of race classification with its crude tests: a pin suddenly into one, and depending on whether you yelped *"Eina"* or *"Aitsho"* for "Ouch," you were classified "colored"—of mixed heritage—or "Bantu"; and the havoc it played with family life when siblings could be assigned to different race groups because some were more swarthy than others. And do you remember that people committed suicide because of race classification? Others played white and would avoid members of their families who were less Caucasian-looking.

Recall the awfulness of the iniquitous pass laws and the migratory labor system and its single-sex hostels and what havoc it caused to black family life in a country that without any sense of irony celebrated Family Day as a public holiday. Isn't it bizarre in the extreme that Nelson Mandela had to wait until he was seventy-six before casting a vote for the very first time in the land of his birth, when whites could do so when they turned eighteen? When I became archbishop in 1986 it was a criminal offense for me to live in the archbishop's official residence in Bishopscourt, Cape Town, because of the Group Areas Act. I told the government I was arch-bishop and would live in my official residence and they could do what they liked and I wasn't asking for their permission. Fortu-nately, they did nothing. But that's where we come from: nearly three million people forcibly removed, as from Sophiatown, which was replaced by the very subtly named Triomf, or Triumph. To rub salt into our wound, Triomf retained many of the street names of the old Sophiatown. How wonderful that the iniquity has been reversed—Triomf is Sophiatown again.

Yes, we come from far, when you had public notices that read, "Natives and dogs not allowed." And those others, "Drive carefully, Natives cross here," which people changed to read, hair-raisingly, "Drive carefully, Natives very cross here"; when they used at elec-tion time to show pictures of an unkempt black and, to stampede whites to vote for them, ask, "Do you want your daughter to marry this man?" Blacks asked, "Show us your daughter first!"

With such antecedents you would have thought the headlines "Vicious race riots in . . ." must surely apply to South Africa. But remarkably, it was not in South Africa that race riots happened, but fairly recently in Manchester, England.

We were the world's most despised pariah. South Africans had to skulk abroad, hiding their nationality. Now we are, I think, still the flavor of the week. Our country through President Thabo Mbeki has been in the forefront of the creation of the African Union and in the conception and promotion of NEPAD and the African renaissance. That is a remarkable turnaround. South Africans proclaim their national identity proudly. Many wear the new flag on their lapels and emblazoned on their luggage. They want everyone to know they come from Madiba-land.[8] Our constitution is widely acclaimed as one of the most liberal and most advanced. Look at the remarkable role our land is playing in peacemaking in Africa, in the Ivory Coast, in Burundi and the Democratic Republic of the Congo, and elsewhere. The prestigious publication *The Economist* in London seriously proposed that President Mbeki should have been this year's Nobel Peace laureate because of his efforts to broker peace in so many of Africa's trouble spots. That's a huge feather in his cap and in our national cap.

And by the way, there are not too many countries that can say they have had four Nobel Peace laureates, as we can. We have two Nobel Literature laureates as well. It was in South Africa that the first heart transplant happened. Our sporting exploits have not been something to sniff at. We have been rugby world champions and hosted the 1995 Rugby World Cup splendidly. We have hosted with panache the World Cricket Cup and the World Golf Cup, which we won. Look at the magnificent exploits of golfers Retief Goosen and Ernie Els. We have won soccer's Africa Nations Cup once and we can do so yet again. And we will be hosting the world's greatest sporting extravaganza, the 2010 World Soccer Cup.

More than seven million people have access now to clean water which they were denied before. And 1.4 million now have electricity available. We have an independent and vociferous press and an outstanding judiciary. These are accomplishments we should celebrate and trumpet abroad far more than we do.

Yes, we do have problems. The most serious is the devastation caused by the ravages of the HIV/AIDS pandemic. Over four million of our people are infected. It is estimated that nearly four hundred thousand South Africans will die this year from AIDS. That is shattering. And yet I want to say that there is something to celebrate even in this awful situation, and it is this: most of the victims are blacks, and you would have thought (given where we come from) that whites would say, "Good riddance to bad rubbish"; quite the contrary, many of the most dedicated, most committed workers in the anti-HIV/AIDS campaign are whites. That is something to celebrate, something to trumpet, and I want to pay a very warm tribute to you, our white compatriots, for your remarkable generosity and dedication.

That is not all. There are many white fellow South Africans out there doing fantastic work. I think of the white ballet dancers who decided they wanted to teach black township kids ballet. They started out ten years ago and formed something called Dance for All; or Angela Rackstraw, a young white woman who is an art therapist and started a project, the Community Art Therapy Program, to work with traumatized, isolated, and abused township youth to help rehabilitate them. I am sure there are many, many others out there, and we salute you for your enthusiasm and dedication.

What Are the Failures and Challenges?

One of the undoubted gifts we bring to the world is our diversity and our capacity to affirm and celebrate our diversity so that today we have eleven official languages. We have a polyglot four-language anthem. We say that each one of us matters and we need each other in the spirit of *ubuntu*, that we can be human only in relationship, that a person is a person only through other persons. Our diversity, which we must affirm and celebrate, is diversity of race, of language, of culture, of religion, and of points of view. We want our society to be characterized by vigorous debate and dissent, where to disagree is part and parcel of a vibrant community—a community in which we play the ball not the person and do not think that those who disagree, who express dissent, are ipso facto disloyal or unpatriotic. An unthinking, uncritical, kowtowing party line-toeing is fatal to a vibrant democracy. I am concerned to see how many have so easily been seemingly cowed and apparently intimidated to comply. I am sure proportional representation has been a very good thing, but it should have been linked to constituency representation.[9] I fear that the party lists have had a deleterious impact on people, even if that was not the intention. It is lucrative to be on a party list. The rewards are substantial, and if calling in question party positions jeopardizes one's chances to get on the list, then not too many are foolhardy, and they opt for silence to become voting cattle for the party.

In the struggle days it was exhilarating because they spoke of a mandate—you had to justify your position in vigorous exchanges.

That seems no longer to be the case. It seems that sycophancy is coming into its own. I would have wished to see far more open debate of, for instance, the HIV/AIDS views of the president in the ANC. Truth cannot suffer from being challenged and examined. There surely can't have been unanimity from the outset. I did not agree with the president, but that did not make me his enemy. He knows that I hold him in high regard, but none of us is infallible; and that is why we are a democracy and not a dictatorship. The government is accountable, as are all public figures, to the people. I would have hoped for far more debate and discussion.

Let us look to the rock from which we are hewn. We should lower the temperature in our public discourse and hopefully thus increase the light. We should not impugn the motives of others but accept the bona fides of all. If we believe in something, then surely we will be ready to defend it rationally, hoping to persuade those opposed to change their point of view. We should not too quickly want to pull rank and to demand an uncritical, sycophantic, obsequious conformity. We need to find ways in which we engage the so-called masses, the people, in public discourse through *indaba*s, town hall forums, so that no one feels marginalized but instead feels that their point of view matters, it counts. Then we will develop a national consensus. We should debate more openly, not using emotive language, issues such as affirmative action, transformation in sport, racism, xenophobia, security, crime, violence against women and children. What do we want our government to do in Zimbabwe? Are we satisfied with quiet diplomacy there? Surely human rights violations must be condemned as such whatever the struggle credentials of the perpetrator. It should be possible to talk as adults about these issues without engaging in slanging matches.

What is black economic empowerment when it seems to benefit not the vast majority but a small elite that tends to be recycled? Are we not building up much resentment that we may rue later? It will not do to say people did not complain when whites were enriched. When were the old regime's standards our standards? And remember that some of the most influential values spoke about "The people shall share."[10] We were involved in the struggle because we believed we would evolve a new kind of society—a caring, a compassionate society. At the moment many, too many, of our people live in grueling, demeaning, dehumanizing poverty. We really must work like mad to eradicate poverty. We should talk about whether spending all that money on arms is morally justifiable in the face of the poverty which poses the most immediate threat to our safety and security. We should discuss as a nation whether BIG—that is, "Basic Income Grant" for the poor—is not really a viable way forward.

We should not be browbeaten by pontificating decrees from on high. We cannot glibly on full stomachs speak about handouts to those who often go to bed hungry. It is cynical in the extreme to speak about handouts when people can become very rich at the stroke of a pen. If those are not massive handouts, then what are? Very few poor people want a handout; they are proud, but they also need a leg up. We should be able to say, while it has been important to build over one million housing units, that many of these are just not acceptable. People call them Unos, like the Italian car. They are our next generation of slums. The public schemes have provided some good models. Habitat for Humanity has shown what is possible. An Irish millionaire every year brings out at his own cost three hundred or so fellow Irish and they build fifty beautiful houses in a week costing R48,000 each. Why can't South Africans do the same?

We want a new quality of society—compassionate, gentle, and caring. The kind of society where the president sits on the floor to talk to his people in their modest house, where the president gives a lift in the presidential cavalcade to a woman so she can attend a presidential reception for Charlize Theron to celebrate her Oscar—actions recently carried out by our president, which says he has a heart as well as a head. It is the kind of society where a widow cups the president's face in the palms of her hands and looks into his eyes after he has spoken movingly in Afrikaans at the funeral of her wonderful husband, Beyers Naudé.[11] The picture of the two of them speaks so eloquently of the kind of nation we want to be: a nation where all belong and know they belong; where all are insiders, none is an outsider; where all are members of this remarkable, this crazy country—they belong in the rainbow nation.

Yes, we are a scintillating success waiting to happen. We will succeed because God wants us to succeed for the sake of God's world. For we are so utterly improbably a beacon of hope for the rest of the world.

Replying to Tutu in an online party newsletter, Mbeki generated more headlines with a vigorous counterattack. He denied silencing dissent, defended his government's policies, accused Tutu of gratu-

itously insulting ANC members, and questioned Tutu's familiarity with the facts and his "respect for the truth." The controversy continued for weeks, with the party publishing a series of ten papers on "The Sociology of the Public Discourse in South Africa." The discussion was described by the ANC as perhaps the most intense political debate of the year, more heated than that around the national election campaign.

CHAPTER 16

What Has Happened to You, South Africa?

The Price of Freedom Is Eternal Vigilance

In 2006, two years after the controversy that concluded the previous chapter, Tutu focused his criticisms on other South African leaders. In 2005 Mbeki had fired South Africa's deputy president, Jacob Zuma, after an associate had been jailed for bribing Zuma during negotiations with European armaments companies bidding for contracts for the government's military rearmament program. Zuma was not immediately prosecuted on arms deal charges, but in 2006, he was charged with raping an HIV-positive woman more than thirty years his junior. He was acquitted after testifying that the sex was consensual but was criticized by the judge for failing to take precautions against being infected. As the ruling party began to discuss successors to Mbeki, forces that had become disenchanted with him—including the ANC's allies in the unions and the Communist Party—coalesced around Zuma.

1

In a lecture given in August 2006, when prosecutors were investigating corruption charges against Zuma, Tutu intervened in the debate over who should succeed Mbeki.[1]

Our political atmosphere that has been remarkably stable given our less than propitious antecedents has recently been convulsed by the succession crisis in the ANC, with cries of plots and conspiracies and all the fallout that has resulted in considerable turbulence. I thought it might not be entirely inappropriate to talk about leadership: true, real leadership.

There is an episode in the Christian Gospels when the disciples of Jesus were bickering about leadership positions. The two brothers James and John, sons of Zebedee, wanted to be a cut above the other ten disciples, so they stole a march on their comrades by approaching their master, asking to be given quite prominent positions—one to sit on either side of Jesus in his glory. You couldn't have asked for anything more exalted. Their ten comrades fumed, but not at the lack of humility on the part of their colleagues. Not on your life. They were upset that the two had got in their claims first and, as it were, beaten them to the draw. It was an unsavory incident as they quarreled publicly about who would be the top dog. You would have thought that people who had been the associates of Jesus would be characterized by attractive qualities, such as humility and modesty. So Jesus called them together to give them a profound lesson on true greatness, real leadership. Just listen:

And when the other ten apostles heard it, they began to be indignant with James and John. But Jesus called them to him and said to them, "You know that those who are recognized as governing and are supposed to rule the Gentiles lord it over them, and their great men exercise authority and dominion over them. But this is not to be so among you; instead, whoever desires to be great among you must be your servant. And whoever wishes to be most important and first in rank among you must be slave of all. For even the Son of Man came not to have service rendered to him, but to serve, and to give his life as a ransom for many.

MARK 10:41–45

Now what kind of advice is that? Totally unrealistic, sentimental, and utopian. They would make mincemeat of you in a hard-nosed, cynical world where it is dog eat dog, survival of the fittest, and everyone for himself in a setting of cutthroat competition. But is that kind of success really what people in fact admire, indeed revere? Mother Teresa has been held in the highest regard, indeed reverence, by very many in our contemporary world. There are many things you could say of her, but macho is certainly not one of them. She is revered not because she was a success. In many ways you could say she failed to stem the tide of poverty whose victims she served so selflessly, and yet she was considered to be a saint in her lifetime. Much the same could be said of a Madiba, of a Dalai Lama, of a Mahatma Gandhi, a Martin Luther King Jr., a Dietrich Bonhoeffer. Thus we cannot rule out of court a priori that seem-

ingly odd piece of advice. People were in awe of the likes of Mother
Teresa because they had given selflessly of themselves, poured out
their lives on behalf of others.

Leading for the Sake of the Led

The formula Jesus propounded clearly was not so utopian and unrealistic. Almost all who have become outstanding leaders have
demonstrated this remarkable attribute of selfless altruism. The
leader is there not for what he or she can get out of this exalted position. No, the real, the true leader knows the position is to enable
the leader to serve those she leads. It is not an opportunity for self-
aggrandizement, but for service of the led. And almost always this
attribute is demonstrated most clearly by the fact that the one who
aspires to lead suffers for the sake of the cause, for the sake of the
people. It is the litmus test of the leader's sincerity, the unambiguous stamp of authenticity of her credentials. Mother Teresa volun-
tarily took the vow of poverty and left the comfort of her European
home to live in the squalor of her new Calcutta slum convent. The
Dalai Lama has been in exile for four decades. Aung San Suu Kyi, a
dainty, petite woman, has made full-grown men armed to the teeth
quake with trepidation, and so they have made her spend ten of the
last seventeen years under house arrest in her Burma homeland.
Mahatma Gandhi left the comforts of a successful legal practice for
his pursuit of *satyagraha,* clad in a skimpy costume, and helped to

make India independent. We could go on in this vein multiplying examples.

It is because of this principle—that suffering in some form validates the authenticity of the leader who is there not for himself but for the led—that almost everywhere the leaders of liberation movements won the first post-independence elections of their countries so easily. They had demonstrated their altruism by being either jailed or exiled or by being involved in other ways in the liberation struggle. Thus an Nkrumah, a Nyerere, a Kenyatta, a Machel, a Seretse Khama, a Nujoma, a Mugabe, a Mandela won in a canter. They passed the first test of a true leader—selfless altruism—with flying colors. Paradoxically, the colonial or oppressive regime were being hoisted with their own petard, for whenever they took action against someone in the struggle, they were putting a stamp of authenticity on their victim.

Integrity

The led—the people, the so-called masses—in a way can be gullible, for they almost always cannot believe that their leaders are not people of integrity, upholding high moral values. I must confess that I have been quite naïve. During the days of our struggle, our people were magnificently altruistic. We had a noble cause and almost everyone involved was inspired by high and noble ideals. When you told even young people that they might be teargassed, hit with quirts,[2] or have vicious dogs set on them, that they might be detained and tortured and even killed, there was a spirit almost of bravado as they said, "So what? I don't care what happens to me as long as it advances our cause." They spoke of their blood watering the tree of our freedom. It was breathtaking stuff—they really meant it, that the cause was the be-all and end-all and they were ready to sacrifice anything, even pay the supreme sacrifice for this cause. My naïveté was that I believed that these noble attitudes and exalted ideals would, come liberation, be automatically transferred to hold sway in the new dispensation. We South Africans were a special breed, and I believed we would show the world, hagridden especially in Africa by the scourge of corruption, that we were a cut above the hoi polloi. Wow! What a comprehensive letdown—no sooner had we begun to walk the corridors of power than we seemed to want to make up for lost time. We succumbed to the same temptations as those others we had thought to be lesser mortals, those others who seemed congenitally unable to keep their hands out of the till. At least we can say it shows we are quite human, that original sin has not passed us by.

How utterly despicable and how thoroughly disillusioning that there have been officials called "civil servants" who have proved to be neither civil nor servants, who have actually robbed the most needy through pocketing their social welfare grants. The victims have been the elderly, robbed of their desperately needed pensions, often the only income in homes where those traditionally the breadwinners are unemployed. Such corrupt persons have shown they are devoid of a sense of shame and common decency. How salutary that the minister responsible has acted decisively and with almost brutal efficiency to bring the culprits to book. Then there have been all the innuendos and allegations about the possible shady aspects in connection with the arms deal, some relating to our former deputy president, but not just him. We do hope that there really will be a thorough investigation, for there are media reports that prosecutors in Germany and France are taking steps that have a bearing on the arms deal.

Last week a newspaper columnist said he thought it was wrong to rule Mr. Jacob Zuma out of the succession race simply because he had been involved in a rape case, had on his own admission committed adultery, and possibly because he had no university education. That columnist contended that quite a few leading political figures were known to have had affairs and have had no university degrees, but this had not stopped them from pursuing an often successful political career. Thus Jacob Zuma should, if he was acquitted in the corruption trial, be permitted to run for the country's presidency by running for that of the ANC. I agree that the lack of a university degree should not be a bar to his being president. But I disagree about the sexual misdemeanor as not posing such an obstacle. So far as I can tell, no politician has campaigned for public office having declared in advance a sexual misdemeanor. Knowledge of such has almost always come much later. More usual has been someone being guilty or suspected of this *after* taking office.

I certainly do not think the misdemeanor as such should necessarily disqualify a candidate. After all, God did not balk at using an adulterer, King David, to be the ancestor par excellence of the

Messiah. The crucial difference is that there was contrition and an asking for forgiveness in the case of David. I am not aware that Mr. Zuma apologized for engaging in what he claims to have been consensual sex, a version accepted by the court which acquitted him. He engaged in casual sex with someone young enough to be his daughter at a time when he had been heading up the government-backed Moral Regeneration Movement of the country. He apologized for his extraordinary claim about the efficacy of taking a shower to ward off HIV/AIDS when he was at one time head of the government's HIV/AIDS campaign.

But all of these pale in the face of the behavior of his supporters outside the court. That conduct was abominable and quite disgraceful. So far as I can tell, at no time does he seem to have been nonplussed or embarrassed by it. His supporters quite rightly demanded that their champion should be presumed innocent until proven guilty. Yet they did not accord the corresponding right to the plaintiff. They vilified and abused her. They intimidated her to such an extent that she had to use a nom de plume to hide her identity, and the police feared for her life to such an extent that they provided her with a round-the-clock guard; and I am not sure whether she has not left our shores, because no one could guarantee that she would not be assaulted and even murdered by incensed supporters. Our constitution, which the country's president promises to guard and uphold, guarantees to each of us the right to our point of view. I like Jacob Zuma as a warm, very approachable person, but he did nothing to stop his supporters. I for one would not be able to hold my head high if a person with such supporters were to become my president. What sort of example would he be setting? I pray that someone will be able to counsel him that the most dignified, most selfless thing—the best thing he could do for a land he loves deeply—is to declare his decision not to take further part in the succession race of his party. I appeal to his undoubted patriotism as demonstrated by his distinguished role in the struggle. The litmus test, as I said at the beginning, is the well-being, the good of the people, and not self-aggrandizement by the leader.

What would prevent the new president from invoking the imperatives of Zulu culture to put damsels in distress out of their misery of what he perceived as their sexual arousal?[3] There surely is conduct that might be tolerated in a lesser mortal but that would be anathema in the head of state. We speak of gravitas—in our language of shadow, *isithunzi,* a presence. We want to experience our head of state as being presidential. He or she is not an ordinary person. People want their leader to have charisma, to be regal and exalted, dignified, almost godlike as expressing the best about their idealized corporate consciousness and identity. But they also want their leader to be a person of flesh and blood, not remote, but down to earth, in touch with them, aware of their aspirations, anguish, and needs, and to know where the shoe pinches.

This tall order is more likely to be accomplished when the system is transparent and accountable. Our present way of electing our president[4] and our parliamentary and provincial and local representatives has served us well in our transitional period. We have held three elections which have been declared free and fair. Foreign observers can hardly hide their boredom at the humdrum routine.

We need to make those elected more accountable to the electorate than to the party bosses who control the party lists. It is high time that our president was elected directly by the people. It is high time that constituencies came into their own so that representatives knew they owed their primary loyalty and accountability to the constituents rather than to the party bosses. Ours would become an even more vibrant, more engaged democracy, because it is still the case that he who pays the piper calls the tune. There would be a more rigorous putting through its paces of the executive branch by its legislative counterpart than is now the case. The party lists tend to foster acquiescence and a supine kowtowing sycophancy. The price of freedom, we have been told times without number, is eternal vigilance. Power is insidious. It can subvert the best of us, and we need help to keep its corrupting attributes from corrupting even the best of us.

A Moral Universe

We inhabit a moral universe where ultimately right and goodness and justice, truth and freedom will always prevail over their ghastly counterparts. It is God's world and God is in charge. The remarkable messengers of God declared God to be notoriously biased in favor of the little ones of this world—the despised, the oppressed, the marginalized, represented in scripture by the triad of the widow, the orphan, and the alien. These prophets told us God had a specially soft spot for the downtrodden and always would act in their behalf against the top dogs, the powerful, the cruel, the hard-hearted; and so their God set free a bunch of slaves, this God acted on behalf of a nonentity, a Naboth against the king. The God for Christians sent God's Son, born in a stable, of the village carpenter and his teenage wife. This Son companied not with presidents and archbishops but with prostitutes and sinners and claimed that we would be judged as worthy or not worthy of heaven by how we treated the hungry, the thirsty, the naked—and, staggeringly, declared that what we did or did not do to them we did or did not do for him.

Yes, power would always be judged by how it treated God's favorites, as we see in Psalm 72 (NEB):

O God, endow the king with thy own justice,
and give thy righteousness to a king's son,
that he may judge thy people rightly
and deal out justice to the poor and suffering.
May hills and mountains afford thy people
peace and prosperity in righteousness.
He shall give judgement for the suffering
and help those of the people that are needy;
he shall crush the oppressor.
He shall live as long as the sun endures,
long as the moon, age after age.
He shall be like rain falling on early crops,
like showers watering the earth.
In his days righteousness shall flourish,

prosperity abound until the moon is no more.
May he hold sway from sea to sea,
from the river to the ends of the earth.
Ethiopians shall crouch low before him;
his enemies shall lick the dust.
The kings of Tarshish and the islands shall bring gifts,
the kings of Sheba and Seba shall present their tribute,
and all kings shall pay him homage,
all nations shall serve him.
For he shall rescue the needy from their rich oppressors,
the distressed who have no protector.
May he have pity on the needy and the poor,
deliver the poor from death;
may he redeem them from oppression and violence
and may their blood be precious in his eyes.
May the king live long
and receive gifts of gold from Sheba;
prayer be made for him continually,
blessings be his all the day long.
May there be abundance of corn in the land,
growing in plenty to the tops of the hills;
may the crops flourish like Lebanon,
and the sheaves be numberless as blades of grass.
Long may the king's name endure,
may it live for ever like the sun;
so shall all peoples pray to be blessed as he was,
all nations tell of his happiness.

Blessed be the Lord God, the God of Israel,
who alone does marvellous things;
blessed be his glorious name for ever,
and may his glory fill all the earth.
Amen, Amen

Always, without exception, those who use power for their own self-advancement, their self-glorification and self-enrichment at the cost of God's favorites, come a cropper. They may strut the world's stage as if they were the cock of the walk, but always, all will bite the dust. Stalin, Hitler, Franco, Amin, et al—where are they now? The perpetrators of the injustice of apartheid seemed to be invincible at the height of their power. Today hardly anyone admits to having supported apartheid. And so we appeal to those who have power in the world, in the Middle East, in Zimbabwe: remember who God's favorites are and that if you act against them you will one day bite the dust, and indeed do so comprehensively.

If you want to be the greatest, then you must be the servant of all. It does not seem to be quite such a crazy piece of advice after all. Let us not become the callous, materialistic and acquisitive, ostentatious society lambasted by President Mbeki in his Mandela lecture last month. May we become the caring, compassionate society in which each one matters, is cherished, counts.

In December 2007 the ANC's five-yearly national conference unceremoniously dumped Mbeki as party leader. Failing to see what a trade union leader had described as the "tsunami" bearing down

on him, Mbeki had sought reelection, hoping to continue as head
of the party and influence the choice of the country's next president.
Zuma defeated him in a landslide, but the party left Mbeki to serve
out his term as president of South Africa. Ten days later, prosecutors
served an indictment on Zuma, setting out charges of racketeering,
money laundering, corruption, and fraud. This began a fifteen-
month legal struggle in which his defense lawyers launched a series
of challenges seeking to exclude evidence and to stop the trial on
technical grounds—and during which the party removed Mbeki
from the presidency and replaced him with an interim president
pending national elections in April 2009. In a parallel process, the
ANC and its allies advocated an ill-defined "political solution" to
remove the prospect of the next president taking office while facing
serious criminal charges.

2

Tutu's unhappiness at the behavior of a liberation movement whose
leaders he had once respected and in support of whom he had
campaigned when their voices had been silenced culminated in the
weeks leading up to the 2009 elections. In March 2009, the gov-
ernment barred the Dalai Lama from entering South Africa for a
peace conference organized by football authorities ahead of the 2010
World Cup soccer tournament. The popular and respected finance
minister, Trevor Manuel, reacted to the resulting uproar by attack-
ing the Dalai Lama's credentials, saying that criticizing the Tibetan

leader was seen in many quarters as "equivalent to trying to shoot Bambi." Tutu told a television interviewer he was flabbergasted.

I'm having a bad dream. I mean, South Africa—we who have been held as such a wonderful example. We have one of the best constitutions in the world—we who have striven so much, with the support of the international community, to have a new kind of society that respected human rights. *We* have done this! I'm sorry: I've just seen what the minister of finance has said. I couldn't believe it! Trevor Manuel! That he could sink so low, that he should say such demeaning, derogatory things about the Dalai Lama. Who is the Dalai Lama? The Dalai Lama, Trevor Manuel, if you don't know, has won the Nobel Peace Prize. Trevor Manuel, if you do not know who the Dalai Lama is, he is one of the very few people in the world who can fill Central Park. This is one of the holiest human beings in the world. He has been in exile for fifty years and has not a bit of anger or resentment against China. He says, We do not want to secede from China; we want autonomy so that our culture, our religion can flourish. That is all he wants. Trevor, I love you—I respected you. I did not believe that I would wake up one day and hear that Trevor Manuel could scrape the bottom of the barrel so appallingly.

I'm disappointed in all that the government has done in relation to this. I'm disappointed in what they've done in relation to Burma; I'm disappointed that they refuse to let the Security Council discuss Zimbabwe.[5] I'm deeply disappointed that you—the government—could disgrace us in this fashion. It's unbelievable. You can't take such disgraceful positions and believe you're taking them on my behalf. You're taking them on your behalf, because China has given you, the ANC, money. Not given our country money, given you—the ANC—money. You have the right to reward them, but don't do it in my name. Don't do it, please, in my name. Don't disgrace us so horrendously.

If you go anywhere today in the world, many of our friends ask, "What has happened to you? What has happened to you, South Africa? We struggled with you and together we won this great victory, and we believed that we didn't have to worry, that South Africa would be on the side of victims, opposing dictators, seeking to uphold human rights." We are destroying our legacy; we have tumbled from the moral high ground. We are the pits.

The trouble with these people in government is that they've got power now and they believe that they're going to have power forever, and you have to keep warning them. The Afrikaner Nationalists thought they were invincible. Let me tell this ANC government what I told the Afrikaner Nationalist government: You may have power now, but you're not God. Remember: you're not God, and one day, you'll get your comeuppance.

3

Three weeks before the April 2009 elections, Tutu addressed a church audience in Zuma's home province of KwaZulu-Natal.

Why was Jesus Christ condemned and killed? Well, it was because he upset the power status quo of his day. He annoyed that religious leadership, the archbishops of the day, because of his appallingly low standards. Have you ever thought about just how low God's standards are, because anyone, everyone can enter heaven, and especially the ones Jesus seemed to delight in meeting. He annoyed the leaders because he sat with prostitutes; he sat with those they called sinners and those who were sellouts, the tax collectors. I mean, can you imagine if you saw me go into the red-light district and go into a brothel? Which of you would say, "No, we know the archbishop; he's going to be preaching the gospel there"? Hey? And yet actually that is where we should be, because that is where our Lord was to be found. Incredible!

And just look at the parents he had. They didn't even have enough clout to get a room in the inn. Somebody told the story of Joseph going to the innkeeper and saying, "Oh, please man, please help me. My wife is pregnant; she's about to have a baby," and the innkeeper says, "It's not my fault," so Joseph says, "It's not mine either."

You know, we make an awful mistake when we think of Jesus as the good shepherd, and see the good shepherd carrying a little fluffy lamb. Because fluffy little lambs never stray from their mommies. The sheep that is likely to stray is that obstreperous, troublesome old ram. The point of the story is that God is prepared to leave ninety-nine perfectly well behaved sheep, to say, "Sorry guys, we know you're already going to heaven, that's fine," and he goes where? To look for this *one,* and he's not going to find it with nice fleece—it's gone through a wire fence, it's fallen into a ditch of dirty water, smelling to high heaven, its fleece is torn. *That* is the sheep the good shepherd goes after and carries on his shoulder. And what does Jesus say? Jesus says, not that there is joy; Jesus says there is *greater* joy over this one than over the ninety-nine. We have here a Jesus who shows an extraordinary bias in favor of those who don't count. He speaks about the Last Judgment, and he says you're going to be judged by how you treat the down-and-outs: the hungry, the thirsty, the naked.

But listen to the bombshell, which you and I hardly ever seem to take seriously. The bombshell is that Jesus all along has been talking about a kind of solidarity; here he says it's an identification: "When you do it to this one, you do it to me." If we had the right kind of eyes, we would look, you would say, "Hey, I fed Jesus." We don't believe this. Just think of the person maybe you despise most of all and then look again, because that's Jesus. It's God. I represent God; you represent God. Are you aware of that?

Jesus in fact was carrying on an incredible tradition. God is not evenhanded. God is biased horrendously. In the book of Exodus God was biased in favor of a bunch—they were not even a people—they were just a rabble of slaves who had done nothing. God chose them freely. Let's read Bibles again, because they're the most explosive things ever. Leviticus talks a lot about ritual, and then in chapter 19, Leviticus says: God says to Moses, "Moses, go and tell those people they must be holy like I am holy." And you think they are talking about ritual holiness, and then you read that chapter and he says, No, no, when you are harvesting, don't harvest everything, leave something for the poor; and constantly God reminds them, behave nicely to the alien because you're an alien. So when you're holy and the people of this God, you are always going to have to be biased in favor of the weak, the poor, the hungry. Do you remember what Isaiah does? They are in church, and can you imagine now—I'm talking as an Anglican—can you imagine in the cathedral, they've got incense and the archbishops and bishops are processing, and they're all holy, and someone comes in there and says, "To hell with these things, man. This is an abomination. I don't want these things; this is a noise I don't like." That's what the prophet Isaiah did: he said, Away with this—when you lift your hands they're full of blood; you are murderers. If you want to be accepted by me, then show it by how you treat the weakest, the widow, the orphan, the alien. You can go on and on and on in that fashion. Don't ask for God's Holy Spirit because it's going to send you to preach the good news to the poor, to proclaim liberty.

My dear sisters and brothers, we were involved in the struggle against injustice. We cared for those whom our Lord called the least of these sisters and brothers. People took incredible risks during that struggle and eventually, with the support of our friends overseas, we won that great victory that was crowned by 1994— our first democratic elections. And we were the flavor of the month around the world. Everybody was thrilled with us. And of course we had this incredible human being, Nelson Mandela, and now everybody wants a piece of him. And we surprised the world too by our Truth and Reconciliation Commission, and people expected that we were going to be moving, as it were, from glory to glory.

We have a constitution that says we outlaw discrimination based on almost all of the things that used to separate people: ethnicity, race, faith—now we say you don't discriminate against people because of disability and certainly not on the basis of their sexuality.

We thought we had arrived and maybe we let our guard down, and now it is tough. My friends, it is tough. God was smart to let me retire when I retired. I'm saying that half-facetiously—*only* half-facetiously. It was one of the easiest things actually, now that I look at it, to be against something. A far more difficult task was left to you: making the reality of our freedom. When our new government behaves somewhat strangely, it is very difficult to condemn, because it looks like you are really unpatriotic. You have a very difficult row to hoe.

We are at a bad place just now in our country. We imagined that the idealism, the altruism, the being concerned about others more than ourselves, all of those things would carry over automatically into the post-apartheid era. We let our guard down, and we were surprised how quickly we seemed to forget. Have you gone to some of our public offices? Have you seen how they treat people? We are behaving in many of those places exactly as they used to behave under apartheid.

I like Jacob Zuma—he's warm, he's friendly—but in the year of Barack Obama, can you imagine what it is like when you're walking in a street in New York and they ask you who is going to be your president? I have to say that at the present time, I can't pretend that I'm looking forward to having Zuma as my president. For his own sake I hope we are not going to have a political solution.[6] If he is innocent, as he has claimed to be, for goodness' sake let it be a court of law that says so.

Dear friends, is this why people died fighting apartheid? Is this why people went into exile? Is this why people were tortured? I'm not a politician—I hope you are aware of that. I'm not looking to be nominated for anything. I'm an old man who wants to go and sit—I want to have some quality time with my wife. But my heart is sore. We said it looks as if there is something wrong with the arms deal. Can we have a judicial inquiry? And we're told, by those who know better, "No, we looked at it; there's nothing wrong." For goodness' sake, if there is nothing wrong, why then be scared to have a judicial inquiry? Why?

This is our country, our beautiful country. Please allow us old people to go to our graves smiling; please don't let us go with broken hearts. Please, please, we have a fantastic country with fantastic people. Why do we want to spoil it?

A week after this address was delivered, prosecutors dropped charges against Jacob Zuma. Two weeks after that, the ANC was returned to power in national elections. The party lost votes in most provinces, but a dramatic leap in support in Zuma's home province of KwaZulu-Natal limited the overall loss to about 4 percent of the vote. Zuma was elected president by Parliament and sworn in early in May 2009.

NOTES

CHAPTER 1: *God Is Clearly Not a Christian*

1. Luke 10: 25–37.
2. See also chapter 7.

CHAPTER 2: *Ubuntu*

1. In Tutu's mother's language, Setswana, *ubuntu* is rendered as *botho,* and the quoted phrase appears as "Motho ke motho ka motho yo mongwe."
2. A leader of South Africa's black consciousness movement, who was killed by police in 1977.

CHAPTER 3: *No Future Without Forgiveness*

1. Recorded in more detail in chapter 9.
2. A fellow Anglican priest.
3. Nelson Mandela's political mentor and fellow prisoner.
4. The facility in which genocide perpetrators were held.

CHAPTER 4: *What About Justice?*

1. This chapter is drawn from lectures delivered in 2004 to the University of Copenhagen and to the Frank Longford Charitable Trust in London.

2. At the time Tutu spoke, former dictator Augusto Pinochet was fighting off attempts in the Chilean courts to strip him of immunity from prosecution for crimes that occurred during his rule.
3. The Pan Africanist Congress.
4. A descendant of the mostly Dutch settlers who were the first Europeans to live in South Africa.
5. A detailed account of Tutu's work in the commission can be found in his book *No Future Without Forgiveness* (Garden City, NY: Image, 2000).
6. "The Mother," Commentaries on The Dhammapada (Twin Lakes, WI: Lotus Press, 2004).

CHAPTER 7: *Freedom Is Cheaper Than Repression*
1. Reflected in chapters 15 and 16.
2. Luwum was murdered by Idi Amin's regime.

CHAPTER 8: *Watch It! Watch It!*
1. Anastasio Somoza Debayle was overthrown in 1979 and replaced by the Frente Sandinista de Liberación Nacional.
2. A reference to sanctions imposed by the Reagan and first Bush administrations in the United States.

CHAPTER 9: *Our Salvation Is of the Jews*
1. Leading Jewish South African lawyer whose performance at the inquest into killing by police of black consciousness leader Steve Biko became the subject of a film and documentaries.
2. A trial in the small town of Delmas, South Africa, in which anti-apartheid leaders were tried and convicted of treason and jailed for terms of between six and twelve years. They were acquitted on appeal in December 1989 after serving a year of their sentences.
3. A reference to John 4:22. The wording is from the King James Version of the Bible; in another translation used by Tutu (the Revised English Bible), it is rendered as "It is from the Jews that salvation comes."
4. Part of the outcry was occasioned by views that Tutu expressed on forgiveness. See chapter 3.
5. Tutu was critical of the British prime minister for not taking a strong enough stand against apartheid.

6. Suzman was an anti-apartheid parliamentarian; Slovo, a leader of the South African Communist Party; and Sachs, an anti-apartheid veteran and judge of the Constitutional Court.
7. Raids based on laws which required black South Africans to carry a pass stating that they had government permission to live and work in an area.

CHAPTER 11: *I Stand Here Before You*
1. The prime minister of white-ruled Rhodesia from 1964 to 1979.
2. Novel by Alan Paton published in 1948.
3. Muzorewa had joined Ian Smith in leading the transitional administration in the country they renamed Zimbabwe-Rhodesia.
4. The name given the policy by its architects in an attempt to render it more respectable in the eyes of the world.
5. Laws compelling black South Africans to carry a pass stating that they were authorized to be in a particular area often had the consequence of separating workers from their families, who were confined to remote rural "homelands" or "Bantustans" (referred to at the end of this excerpt).

CHAPTER 12: *Utterly Diabolical*
1. The Herstigte Nasionale Party, or Purified National Party, a right-wing breakaway from the governing National Party.
2. A reference to the fact that one of Botha's cabinet ministers had suggested that "apartheid is dead."
3. That is, six South African rands.
4. Piet Koornhof, the cabinet minister responsible for black South Africans.
5. A reference to the Anglo-Boer War of 1899–1902.

CHAPTER 13: *Unbiblical, Unchristian, Immoral, and Evil*
1. Apartheid security forces crossed South Africa's borders to kill African National Congress activists based in Maputo, Mozambique, and Maseru, Lesotho.

CHAPTER 14: *We Must Turn the Spotlight on Ourselves*
1. A recently revealed military death squad which had been named the "Civilian Cooperation Bureau."

2. As noted earlier, the pass laws denied families the right to live together, often forcing workers to live in hostels in urban areas, leaving their families behind in the Bantustans.

3. The followers of the Inkatha Freedom Party, a major force at the time in the province of KwaZulu-Natal, insisted on their right to carry "traditional weapons."

4. Anti-apartheid activists refused to observe police controls on demonstrations because they were used to suppress peaceful protest.

5. A right-wing, pro-apartheid white opposition leader.

6. The Afrikaner Weerstandsbeweging, or Afrikaner Resistance Movement.

7. A priest of the Community of the Resurrection, an English monastic order, who was one of Tutu's earliest mentors. He later became a bishop, an archbishop, and also head of the Anti-Apartheid Movement in Britain.

CHAPTER 15: *Naught for Your Comfort*

1. Nguni languages include isiZulu and isiXhosa, the mother tongue of 40 percent of South Africans—and of Mandela, Mbeki, and Jacob Zuma (the country's president since 2009), as well as of Tutu.

2. The title came from a line in G. K. Chesterton's epic poem "Ballad of the White Horse."

3. NEPAD—the New Partnership for Africa's Development—is an initiative adopted in 2001 in which Mbeki played a leading role; its purpose is to end poverty and promote growth in Africa by promoting good governance.

4. In 2008, African migrants living in poor communities across South Africa were driven out, and many killed, in xenophobic attacks.

5. The 1994 genocide was perpetrated by Hutu extremists, who killed the Tutsi and moderate Hutu.

6. The general secretary of the South African Communist Party, assassinated in 1993.

7. A law that forbade interracial sex.

8. Nelson Mandela's clan name, by which he is affectionately known in South Africa, is Madiba.

9. Members of Parliament are chosen from a list compiled by party leaders on the basis of the proportion of the national vote their party receives. A legislator's seat thus depends on a party committee's decision, not on the vote of local constituents.

10. An allusion to a phrase in the ANC's 1955 landmark policy document, the Freedom Charter.
11. An Afrikaner anti-apartheid and church leader.

CHAPTER 16: *What Has Happened to You, South Africa?*
1. The lecture was delivered in memory of Harold Wolpe, who had been put on trial with Nelson Mandela in 1963 but who escaped from prison and went into exile two months before the trial began.
2. Whips used by police.
3. Zuma was reported to have told the judge who heard the rape trial that the plaintiff was sexually aroused and that, according to Zulu culture, "you can't just leave a woman if she is ready."
4. The president is elected by Parliament.
5. During a two-year term on the UN Security Council, South Africa voted with China and Russia against a resolution condemning human rights violations in Burma and helped block debate on the crisis in Zimbabwe.
6. That is, a political solution to Zuma's prosecution for corruption.

INDEX

Tutu's Tel Aviv visit (1999), 101;
Tutu's three options for, 107
Ivory Coast, 189

Jeremiah, xi
Jesus: activist mandate of, 130,
137–38, 151, 158, 161–63; black
theology and, 120–21, 122; cause
of condemnation and execution,
213; as champion for the vulnerable and oppressed, 60–62, 76,
213–14; Christianity and, 17–18;
crucifix in Church of Sant'Egidio,
Rome, 4; death on the cross, 64,
66; forgiveness and, 27; inclusiveness and, 56, 159; on leadership
as service, 198–200; lowly birth
of, 75, 92, 207; Old Testament
references, 13; parable of the Good
Samaritan, 4; parable of the Last
Judgment, 130, 137; penitent thief
and, 44; as Prince of Peace, 8, 91,
92; purpose for, 126; revelation of
God in, 10–11, 14–15; Zacchaeus
the tax collector and, 31
Jewish Defense League, 96
Jews and Judaism: criticism of Tutu,
94, 95–101, 102, 109; guestbook,
Yad Vashem, Jerusalem (1989),
94; inclusiveness of Yahweh, 14;
Israeli-Palestinian conflict, 85–109;
as a light to nations, 94; revelation of God to, 12, 13–14; roots of
Christianity and, 85–86, 97, 220n
3; sin and God's grace, 9; striving
for kingdom of heaven and, 67; as
supporters, civil rights and anti-

apartheid struggle, 87, 104; Torah's
law of an eye for an eye, 106, 168;
Tutu's press statement, Cincinnati, Ohio (1990), 27; Tutu's press
statement, Jerusalem's Holocaust
Museum (1989), 26; Tutu's remarks
to Gottschalk delegation, Cincinnati (1990), 96–100; Tutu's speech,
Stephen Wise Free Synagogue,
NYC (1989), 85–90. *See also* Israel
Job, 124
John: *1:1*, 11; *1:5*, 156; *1:9*, 9; *4:22*,
220n 3; *5:8–14*, 162; *10:10*, 126;
12:24, 61; *12:32*, 56, 159; *14:6*, 9
1 John: *3:17*, 147; *3:18*, 147; *4:7*, 147;
4:20, 129
John, St., 146–47
John the Apostle, St., 156
justice: restorative, 32, 42–43, 45–47;
retributive, 41, 42, 51; Truth
and Reconciliation Commission,
38–47; Tutu's acceptance speech,
honorary degree, Benin (1991), 32;
Tutu's comment, to Kerry Kennedy
(1998), 37–38; *ubuntu* and, 44

Kafity, Samir, 90, 94
Kant, Immanuel, 10
Kennedy, Kerry, 37–38
kenosis (self-emptying), 121
Kentridge, Sydney, 86, 220n 1
Kenya, 71
King, Martin Luther Jr., 15, 51,
168, 199
1 Kings: *18:17–39*, 68–69; *21*, 161
King's College, London, 113
Koornhof, Piet, 145, 221n 4